Gein

By Scott E. Bowser

ISBN 978-1-63877-080-0
Second Printing May 2021

To my family and friends who stuck by me through the

rough and the good times.

A special thank you to my friends Keith and Lori

for their help in the research for this book.

Jean, thank you for all your help editing this book.

My book would not be what it is without your input and support.

Index

Preface

The story of Ed Gein has had a lasting impact on popular culture as evidenced by its numerous appearances in movies, music and literature. Gein's story was adapted into several movies, including *Deranged* (1974), *In the Light of the Moon* (2000 later retitled *Ed Gein* for the U.S. market), and *Ed Gein: The Butcher of Plainfield* (2007). Gein influenced the nature of book and film characters, most notably such fictional serial killers as Norman Bates (*Psycho*), Leatherface (*The Texas Chainsaw Massacre*), and Buffalo Bill (*The Silence of the Lambs*).

Ed Gein remained for many years a boogeyman figure in much of America. His crimes still resonate today as an example of the nightmarish consequences that can result from a warped childhood.

Ed showed no signs of remorse or emotion during the many hours of interrogation. When Ed talked about the murders and his grave robbing escapades, he spoke very matter-of-factly, even cheerfully at times. He had no concept of the enormity of his crimes.

Chapter 1

Ed Gein

Ed Gein

Edward Theodore Gein was born on Monday, August 27, 1906 at 11:00 pm in the Gein household located at 912 Gould Street in La Crosse, Wisconsin.

Ed's father was George Phillip Gein. George was born on Monday, August 4, 1873 in Bergen, Wisconsin. George's original surname was Gee, so he went by the name of George Gee. He later changed his last name to Gein. George became an orphan at an early age after his parents and sister died in a flooding accident. After the tragedy, George was then adopted by his Uncle Leonhardt from his mother's side of the family.

Ed's mother, Augusta was born Sunday, July 21, 1878. Augusta grew up on a farm outside of La Crosse, Wisconsin. She spoke English, German and played the accordion. Augusta grew up in a strong Lutheran household.

George and Augusta were married on December 4, 1899 at the Chaseburg Vernon County Lutheran Church. They rented a 2 bedroom, 1 bathroom, 922 sq. ft. home located at 1032 Charles Street in La Crosse, Wisconsin.

Ed had one older brother named Henry. Henry was born on Friday, January 17, 1902.

In 1898, George and Augusta moved into a 4 bedroom, 1 bathroom, 1336 sq. ft. home located at 1931 Wood Street in La Crosse, Wisconsin. It is unknown if they owned or rented this home. They did move once more into a 2 bedroom, 1 bathroom, 966 sq. ft. home located at 612 Gould Street. It was at the Gould Street home where Ed Gein was born in 1906.

In 1909, George and Augusta bought the former Schultz Grocery Store and renamed it into A. Gein Mercantile. The mercantile store was located at 914 Caledonia Street, in La Crosse, Wisconsin. Since that time, the mercantile store has been torn down and replaced with a storage building. Augusta kept the store in her name because of George's issue with drinking and spending. George drank excessively; he verbally and physically abused Augusta and his sons.

In 1913, at age seven, Ed and his family moved to a cattle farm located in Camp Douglas, Wisconsin.

In 1914, when Ed was 8 years old, Augusta decides to move to Plainfield, Wisconsin. Augusta purchased a 195-acre farm located at N5691 Second Avenue. Her goal was to move away from the immorality of the city and the sinners that inhabited it. Ed and Henry attended Roche-A-Cri Grade School, a tiny one-room building with 12 students.

When not in school, Ed Gein spent most of his time doing chores on the farm. Augusta was a fervent Lutheran. She preached to her boys the innate immorality of the world, the evil of drinking and the belief that all women (herself excluded) were prostitutes and instruments of the devil. She reserved time every afternoon reading the bible to the boys, usually selecting graphic verses from the Old Testament dealing with death, murder and divine retribution.

With an effeminate demeanor, Ed became a target for bullies. Classmates and teachers recalled off-putting mannerisms such as seemingly random laughter, as if he were laughing at his own jokes. To make matters worse, his mother Augusta would scold him whenever he tried to make new friends. Despite Ed's poor social development, he did well in school, particularly in reading. Ed also learned to play the violin, accordion and the mouth organ.

Both Henry and Ed tried to make their mother happy, but she was rarely pleased with her sons. She often abused them, believing that they were destined to become failures like their father. During their teens and early adulthood, the boys remained detached from people outside of their farmstead; they only had each other for company.

In 1920, Ed graduated from eighth grade and then dropped out of school when he was 14 years old.

On April 1, 1940, Ed's father, George Gein dies of a heart attack and pneumonic fluid in his lungs at the age of 66. Ed was 34 years old at the time, while his brother Henry was 39.

After the death of their father, Ed and Henry began working at odd jobs to financially support the farm and their mother. Ed looked up to his brother Henry and saw him as a hard worker and a man of strong character. Ed tried to emulate his brother's work habits and both brothers were considered reliable and honest by residents of the community. They mostly worked as handymen, yet Ed frequently babysat for neighbors. He enjoyed babysitting, seeming to relate more easily to children than adults. During this time, Henry began to reject his mother's view of the world and began to see a widowed woman who had one child. Augusta was upset over this relationship. Henry started to speak ill of his mother around Ed, which bothered Ed.

In 1942, Ed was eligible for the draft and had to travel away from the farm for the first time by himself to Milwaukee, Wisconsin. He was rejected for the service due to a growth over his left eye which slightly impaired his vision. Henry was also rejected because of his age.

Henry was worried about Eddie's unhealthy attachment to their mother. On several occasions, Henry openly criticized their mother, something that shocked his brother. Ed saw his mother as pure goodness and was mortified that Henry did not see her in the same way. It was possible these incidents led to the untimely and mysterious death of Henry in 1944.

On May 16, 1944, both Henry and Ed were out fighting a brush fire on Henry's land which was just down the road from the Gein farmland. Reportedly, the brothers were separated, and as night fell, Ed lost sight of his brother. When the fire was exhausted, Ed reported to the police that his brother was missing. When the search party was organized, Ed led them directly to his missing brother, who lay dead on the ground. Police had concerns about the circumstances under which the body was discovered. The ground on which Henry lay was untouched by fire, and he had bruises on his head. Despite this, the police dismissed the possibility of foul play. The coroner listed asphyxiation as the cause of death. Although some investigators suspected that Ed Gein killed his brother, no charges were filed against him. Ed was 38 years old and finally, he had his mother all to himself.

In late 1944 Augusta suffered a debilitating stroke brought on by the death of Henry. Ed must now physically take care of his mother. On December 29, 1945, Augusta suffers another stroke and dies from complications from the stroke. Now Ed was truly alone as he lost his best friend. Ed remains on the farm, supporting himself with earnings from odd jobs. He boards up rooms previously used by his mother, including the entire upstairs, the downstairs parlor and living room, leaving them untouched. He lives in a small room next to the kitchen. Ed is now 39 years old and has become interested in reading death cult magazines, adventure stories and war time magazines on the Nazi's and their crimes.

In February 1947, eighteen months after Augusta died, Ed is driven by intense loneliness and what he later claimed to be strange visions, begins to think he could raise the dead by his own will. Ed admits to trying to dig up his own mother but could not because the soil was too sandy. So Ed starts to scout local newspaper obituaries for dead bodies who remind him of his mother. At the age of 41 years old, Ed goes to Spirit Land Cemetery and digs up Grace Beggs, his first corpse.

Ed takes a piece of re-rod and pushes it down until it hit the wood casket. He was able to tell it is wood by tapping the re-rod on top of the casket. Ed discovers he can break into wood caskets but not the other types. The boards on the casket were straight across so Ed did not have to remove all the boards to get at his victim.

On Wednesday, March 29, 1950, Elsie Sparks passes away at the age of 55. She becomes the 2nd corpse that Ed removes from the Plainfield Cemetery.

About this time, Ed does some thresher work for Elmo Ueeck, who lived next door to Cliff Bates. Ed also made extra money by leasing out his land for $10.00 a year. Some of the people who leased Ed's land never paid him. Ed was upset and felt taken advantage of by these people because they never paid him.

Ed babysat for Lester and Irene Hill's son Billy. Ed and Billy became good friends during this time. The Hill family lived at N6520 3rd Street in Plainfield, Wisconsin. Interestingly, Lester Hill used to bully Ed Gein while they were in school.

Ed's third corpse that he removes from Plainfield Cemetery is the body of Marie Bergstrom. Marie passed away on Tuesday, February 6, 1951 at the age of 85.

On Sunday, April, 15, 1951, Mabel Everson passes away at 6:30 pm at the age of 69. Mabel becomes the fourth body that Ed removes from the Plainfield Cemetery. Ed Gein later admitted he felt guilty about taking Mabel's body. He ended up returning to the gravesite and reburied some of the body parts just below the surface.

On Saturday, November 29, 1952, Ursula Jane Callanan passed away and was buried in the Plainfield Cemetery. Ed was 46 years old and Ursula became the sixth body that he had dug up.

In 1953, Ed went to Hancock Cemetery in Hancock, Wisconsin to dig up Lola Foster, the seventh body.

In 1954, Ed was known for frequenting The Fox Head Bar in Babcock, Wisconsin. Mary Hogan owned the bar and was known for being a rough foul-mouthed talking woman. She was a heavier set woman similar in shape to Ed's mother Augusta.

On Wednesday, December 8, 1954, Ed returns to The Fox Head Bar at closing. As Ed walks in the door, he pulls out a .32 caliber pistol and shoots Mary Hogan in the head, killing her. Ed puts Mary's body in the back of his 1938 Chevy pickup and takes her back to his farm. Later that morning, Seymour Lester walks into The Fox Head Bar and discovers blood all over the floor. Police also discovered that $1,500 was missing from the bar as well. Later when the police searched Ed's farm, they discovered a skin-face mask was created from Mary Hogan's face. No other remains of hers were ever identified.

The morning of November 15, 1957 was the opening day of the gun deer season. Ed arrived at Worden's Hardware Store located at 406 Poplar Street in Plainfield, Wisconsin. Ed needed some antifreeze for his car, so Bernice Worden filled up Ed's jar and wrote the sales transaction down in the ledger book. Ed took the antifreeze out to his car and returned to the store. He asked Bernice if he could see the .22 caliber rifle in the gun rack as he was interested in trading in one of his guns for it. While Ed looked at the rifle, Bernice went to look out the window facing the gas station across the street. Ed pulled a .22 caliber bullet from his jacket pocket, loaded it into the rifle and shot Bernice Worden in the back of the head, killing her.

Ed dragged Bernice's body to the rear of the store and onto the loading dock. He placed her body into the back of the Worden Hardware delivery pick up and drove it to East Road where he parked it in the pine trees. Ed walked back to the hardware store, where his car was parked. Then Ed drove his car out to East Road where the Worden's truck was parked. He then loaded Bernice Worden's lifeless body into his trunk and drove home. On his way back to the farm, Ed drove by Lars Thompson who had just shot a deer on Ed's property. Ed never stopped to talk to Lars.

Meanwhile, Bernice's son Frank Worden came to town and stopped at the Phillips 66 gas station to talk to owner Bernard Mushinsky. Both commented that it was odd that the hardware store was closed at 9:30 am. Frank Worden went over to see if his mother was alright. As he walked into the store, he noticed a pool of blood on the floor. Frank immediately called the local sheriff to come at once. At the time, Frank Worden was a Plainfield Deputy Sheriff and a Fire Warden. Frank told local Sheriff Arthur Schley that it had to be Ed Gein who had taken his mother, as Ed was in earlier buying antifreeze.

Sheriff Arthur Schley and Captain Lloyd Schoephoester, from the Green Lake Sheriff Department went out to Ed Gein's farm to question him on the disappearance of Bernice Worden. When the officers arrived at the farm, they never checked if Ed was there. Instead they walked around the back to see if there was a door open. The officers found the door to the woodshed was able to be opened and they entered woodshed. Upon searching Gein's property, the officers discovered Bernice Worden's decapitated body in the woodshed. She was hung upside down by ropes on her wrists, with a crossbar at her ankles. The torso was "dressed out" like that of a deer. Her head was found in a burlap sack with nails hammered through each ear and tied together with twine, as if in readiness for the head to be hung up as a trophy. She had been shot with a .22-caliber rifle and the mutilations were performed after her death.

Sheriff Schley put out an all-points bulletin to find and arrest Ed Gein for the murder of Bernice Worden.

Ed Gein was enjoying a pork chop dinner prepared at the home of Lester and Irene Hill, N6520 3rd Street when they heard the commotion in Plainfield. Ed and Bobby Hill decided they wanted to take a ride into Plainfield to see what was going on. They got into Ed's Maroon 1949 Ford sedan and were just getting into the car when a patrol car pulled in behind them. Ed was taken into custody around 7:30 pm by Sheriff Arden Spees and Deputy Dan Chase and was taken to the Waushara County Jail in Wautoma, Wisconsin. Ed's car sat in Lester Hill's driveway for three days after Ed's arrest.

The Wisconsin State Crime Lab was called in to investigate Ed's farm. Searching the house, authorities found:

- Four noses
- Whole human bones and fragments
- Nine masks of human skin
- Bowls made from human skulls
- Ten female heads with tops sawed off
- Human skin covering several chairs and seats
- Mary Hogan's head in a paper bag

- Bernice Worden's head in a burlap sack
- Nine vulvas in a shoe box
- Skulls on his bedposts
- Organs in the refrigerator
- A pair of lips on a draw string for a window shade
- A belt made from female nipples
- A lampshade made from the skin from a human face
- Found a quantity of formaldehyde and an embalming needle

When questioned, Gein told investigators that between 1947 and 1952, he made as many as 40 nocturnal visits to three local graveyards to exhume recently buried bodies while he was in a "daze-like" state. On about 30 of those visits, he said he had come out of the daze while at the cemetery, left the grave in good order, and returned home empty handed.

On other occasions, Gein said he dug up the graves of recently buried middle-aged women he thought resembled his mother. He took the bodies' home, where he tanned their skins to make his paraphernalia. Gein admitted robbing nine graves and later led investigators to their locations.

Shortly after his mother's death, Gein decided he wanted a sex change and began to create a "woman suit" so he could pretend to be a female. Gein's practice of donning the tanned skin of women was described as an "insane transvestite ritual". Gein denied having sex with the bodies he exhumed, explaining, "They smelled too bad." During the interrogation, Gein also admitted to the shooting death of Mary Hogan, the tavern owner missing since 1954.

Bobby Hill, the 16-year-old youth whose parents were friends with Gein and who attended ball games and movies with him, reported that he was aware of the shrunken heads. Ed Gein had described the heads as relics from the Philippines sent by a cousin who had served in World War II. Upon investigation by the police, these heads were determined to be human facial skin carefully peeled from cadavers and used as masks by Gein.

Waushara County Sheriff Art Schley allegedly physically assaulted Gein during questioning by banging Gein's head and face into a brick wall at the jail, causing Gein's initial confession to be ruled inadmissible.

In December 1968, Schley died of a heart attack at the age of 43, only a month after testifying at Gein's trial. Many who knew him said he was traumatized by the horror of Gein's crime and that this, along with the fear of having to testify (especially about assaulting Gein), led to his early death. One of his friends said, "He was a victim of Ed Gein as if he had bothered him".

On November 22, 1957, Gein was arraigned on one count of first-degree murder in Waushara County Court in front of Judge Boyd Clark. Gein entered a plea of not guilty by reason of insanity. Found mentally incompetent and thus unfit for trial, Gein was sent to the Central State Hospital for The Criminally Insane (now the Dodge Correctional Institution), a maximum-security facility in Waupun, Wisconsin, and was later transferred to the Mendota State Hospital in Madison, Wisconsin.

On November 23, 1957, the psychologist and psychiatrist who interviewed Ed asserted that he was schizophrenic.

On November 24, 1957, the graves of Eleanor Adams and Marie Bergstrom were exhumed. Both caskets were found empty.

On November 29, 1957, deputies found more bones in a 40-foot trench on Ed Gein's Farm.

On December 17, 1957, the judge received a packet from the Central State Hospital stating that Ed was insane and should be permanently committed to the hospital.

On January 6th, 1958, Ed had a sanity hearing in Wisconsin Rapids. He was declared legally insane by Judge Herbert Bunde. He was recommitted to the Central State Hospital.

When investigators revealed the facts about what was found on Ed Gein's farm, the news spread quickly. Reporters from all over the world flocked to the small town of Plainfield, Wisconsin. The town became known worldwide and Ed Gein reached celebrity-like status. People were repulsed, and yet at the same time drawn to the atrocities that took place on Ed Gein's farm.

Psychologists from around the world attempted to find out what made Ed tick. During the 1950's, he gained notoriety as being one of the most famous of documented cases involving a combination of necrophilia, transvestism and fetishism.

Back in Plainfield, residents endured the onslaught of reporters who disrupted their daily lives by bombarding them with questions about Ed. However, many of them eventually became involved in the mania surrounding Ed and contributed whatever information they had. The town of Plainfield is now known around the world as the home of the infamous Ed Gein. Most residents, who knew Ed, only had good things to say about him, other than that he was a little peculiar, had a quirky grin and a strange sense of humor. They never suspected him of being capable of committing such ghastly crimes. But the truth was hard to escape. The little shy, quiet man the town thought they knew was in fact, a murderer who also violated the graves of friends and relatives.

After Gein spent a period of 30 days in the mental institution and was evaluated as mentally incompetent, he could no longer be tried for first degree murder. The people of Plainfield immediately voiced their anger that Ed would not be tried for the death of Bernice Worden. Yet, there was little the community could do to influence the court's decision. Ed was sentenced to the mental institution and his farm went up for auction along with some of his other belongings.

On March 20, 1958 at 2:30 am Ed Gein's farm was burned to the ground by a mysterious fire. Arson was suspected, and a lot of people pointed the finger at the Fire Warden Frank Worden. When Ed Gein heard of the incident, he shrugged his shoulders and said, "Just as well".

On March 30, 1958, everything from the fire was auctioned off. Ed's 1949 Maroon Ford Sedan, which he used to haul the bodies of his victims, was sold at a public auction for $760 to carnival sideshow operator, Bunny Gibbons. Gibbons later charged $.25 to see it.

Ed's blue 1938 Chevy pickup was sold for $215 to Chet Seales (Chet's Wrecker Service).

After spending ten years in the mental institution, the courts finally decided Gein was competent to stand trial. The proceedings began Monday, January 22, 1968, to determine whether Eddie was guilty or not by reason of insanity, for the murder of Bernice Worden. The actual trial began on Thursday, November 7, 1968.

Gein watched as seven witnesses took to the stand. Several of those who testified were lab technicians who performed the autopsy on Bernice Worden. Evidence was heavily stacked against Gein and one a week later the judge reached his verdict. Ed Gein was found guilty of first-degree murder. However, because Gein was found to have been insane at the time of the killing, he was later found not guilty by reason of insanity and acquitted. Soon after the trial, he was escorted back to Central State Hospital for The Criminally Insane.

The families of Bernice Worden, Mary Hogan and the families of those whose graves were raided would never feel justice was served. They believed Gein escaped the punishment that was due to him, but there was nothing more they could do to reverse the court's decision.

Gein would remain at the mental institution for the rest of his life where he spent his days happily and comfortably.

Ed was happy at the hospital – happier perhaps, than he had ever been in his life. He got along well enough with the other patients, though for the most part he kept to himself. Ed was eating three square meals a day (the newsmen were struck by how much heavier he looked since his arrest five years before). Ed continued to be an avid reader. He liked his regular chats with the staff psychologists and enjoyed the handicraft work he was assigned – stone polishing, rug making and other forms of occupational therapy. Ed even developed an interest in ham radios and had been permitted to use the money he had earned to order inexpensive receivers.

All in all, Ed was a perfectly amiable, even docile patient, one of the few in the hospital who never required tranquilizing medications to keep his craziness under control. Indeed, apart from certain peculiarities – the disconcerting way he would stare fixedly at nurses or other female staff members who wandered into his line of vision, it was hard to tell that he was crazy at all.

On Thursday, June 27th, 1974 Ed filed a petition with the Waushara County Clerk of Courts claiming he was now recovered from his mental illness and was fully competent and wanted to be released.

A judge reviewed Ed's petition and ordered a re-examination. The judge rejected Ed's petition and he was returned to the hospital. Ed was 68 years old.

In 1978, at the age of 72 years old, Ed was moved to the Mendota Mental Institute in Madison, Wisconsin. On Thursday, July 26th, 1984, Ed had grown senile after a long battle with cancer and died of respiratory failure in the geriatric ward at Mendota. Ed was 78 years old at the time of his passing.

On Friday, July 27, 1984 at 4pm, Ed Theodore Gein was buried by Bennie and Betty Petrusky in a blue casket, between his mother and brother.

In 2000, Ed Gein' gravestone was stolen. In June 2001, the gravestone was recovered in Seattle, Washington. The gravestone was never put back on Ed's grave, but has been stored in the basement of one of the Plainfield Cemetery board members.

Chapter 2

Bodies Dug Up

Confirmed Bodies Dug Up

Passed Date	Name	Age	Cemetery
February 2, 1947	Grace Beggs	85	Spirit Land
March 29, 1950	Elise L Sparks	55	Plainfield
February 6, 1951	Karin M. Bergstrom	85	Plainfield
May 15, 1951	Mabel C Everson	69	Plainfield
August 26, 1951	Eleanor Adams	52	Plainfield
November 29, 1952	Ursula J Calanan	74	Plainfield
February 17, 1953	Lola E Foster	65	Hancock
November 22, 1955	Harriet A Sherman	70	Plainfield
November 28, 1956	Alzaida B Abbott	73	Spirit Land

Other Possible Bodies

Disappeared	Name	Age	Missing From
October 24, 1953	Evelyn Hartley	15	La Crosse, WI
May 1, 1947	Georgia J. Weckler	8	Fort Atkinson, WI
November 1, 1952	Victor Travis	42	Plainfield, WI
November 1, 1952	Ray Burgess	?	Plainfield, WI
November 28, 1956	Alzaida B. Abbott	73	Spirit Land, WI

Murdered Victims

Murder Date	Name	Age	Location
December 8, 1954	Mary Hogan	53	Babcock, WI
November 16, 1957	Bernice Worden	57	Plainfield, WI

Grace Beggs

Sometime between Sunday, February 9 and Monday, February 10, 1947, Ed Gein dug up Grace Beggs, his first body.

Grace Beggs was born Friday, September 21, 1877 in Mount Morris, Illinois. She was the daughter of John T. Sr. and Grace Tamminga. Grace's parents were married on Monday, December 16, 1872 in Oregon, Illinois. Little is known about what the Tamminga family did for employment or their way of life back then. John Sr. was born Thursday, December 3, 1840 and passed away Tuesday, April 18, 1911 at the age of 70. His wife Grace was born in 1851 and passed away on Saturday, August 7, 1937 at the age of 85. Both are buried at North Deerfield Cemetery in Hancock, Wisconsin.

Grace had 8 brothers and sisters. Arthur, who served in World War 1, was born Sunday, February 4, 1894 and passed away Tuesday, May 7, 1985. He is buried in North Deerfield Cemetery in Hancock, Wisconsin. George was born on Tuesday, September 9, 1879 and passed away in 1948. He is buried at Plum City Union Cemetery in Plum City, Wisconsin. James Jacob was born Saturday, August 20, 1887 and passed away in 1979 at the age of 92. John Jr. was born in 1875 and passed away in 1967. Mike was born May 12, 1885 and passed away in July 1940. William was born Thursday, February 5, 1891 and passed away in 1946 at the age of 55. Jeannie Tamminga Bishop was born on August 1, 1881 and passed away in 1957 at the age of 76. Martha Tamminga Ellerman was born on January 20, 1882 and passed away Tuesday, September 14, 1965. She was known as "Hawkie", and is buried at Plum Lake Cemetery in Sayner, Wisconsin.

The Tamminga family lived at 2230 Lincoln Street, in Pinegrove, Wisconsin, where Grace Beggs went to school until 8th grade in Pinegrove, Wisconsin. After Grace was out of school, she was employed as a housekeeper. She married Myron Wyatt Beggs on Friday, March 6, 1903 when she was 25 years old. Myron was born June 11, 1876 and passed away Monday, January 17, 1966 at age of 89. Both Myron and Grace are buried at Spirit Land Cemetery in Plainfield, Wisconsin.

Grace and Myron had 7 children, 5 boys and 2 girls. Arleigh R was born Friday, November 22, 1907 in Almond, Wisconsin and passed away Sunday, May 23, 1920 at the age of 13. He is buried next to his mom and dad in Spirit Land Cemetery in Plainfield, Wisconsin. Bernard Roy was born Thursday, February 15, 1906 and passed away Tuesday, April 14, 1968 at the age of 62 from a heart attack. Earl G was born Monday, December 11, 1922. He passed away Monday, September 11, 2000 at the age of 77 and is buried at Spirit Land Cemetery in Plainfield, Wisconsin. Herbert was born on Tuesday, June 6 and passed away April 27, 1988 at the age of 71. He is buried at Spirit Land Cemetery in Plainfield, Wisconsin. Orilla Susan Beggs was born Friday, June 19, 1903 and passed away Tuesday, March 25, 1997 at the age of 94. Orilla is buried with her husband at Greenville Cemetery in Belmont, Wisconsin. Roland Herbert Beggs was born November 7, 1904 and passed away on Monday, March 19, 1906 from drinking a large quantity of Strychnine left out by his father (ref March 22, 1906 Appleton Post Crescent). Roland was 2 years old at the time of his death and is buried at Spirit Land Cemetery in Plainfield, Wisconsin.

Grace had 10 grandchildren and passed away from a heart attack on Tuesday, February 4, 1947 at the age of 69. Her funeral services were held at 1:30 pm on Sunday, February 9, 1947 and was laid to rest at 2:00 pm in Spirit Land Cemetery.

Elise Lavina Sparks

Elise Sparks was the second body Ed Gein dug up. Elise was born Sunday, June 10, 1894 and passed away Wednesday, March 29, 1950. She was 55 years old at the time of her death.

Her husband Bert Sparks was born in 1895 and passed away in 1976.They were married Tuesday, January 1, 1918. Bert and Elise had two daughters, Stella and Florence. They all lived on a farm in Plainfield, Wisconsin. Both are buried in Plainfield Cemetery.

Karin Marie Bergstrom

Karin Bergstrom was the third body Ed Gein dug up. Karin was born on Sunday, March 4, 1866 and passed away on Tuesday, February 6, 1951 at St. Mary's Hospital in Racine, Wisconsin. Her husband Nels was born in 1859 and passed away in 1934. They had three sons, Albert, Alfred and Ernest, and three daughters, Emma, Edna and Bessie. Both Nels and Karin are buried in the Plainfield Cemetery.

Karin Marie Bergstrom

Mabel Cornelia Everson

Mabel Cornelia Everson was the fourth body Ed Gein dug up. Mabel was born on Wednesday, June 7, 1882 and passed away on Sunday, April 15th, 1951 at 6:30 pm at the age of 69 following an illness from heart trouble.

Mrs. Everson was born in the town of Oasis in Waushara County. She had three daughters, Mamie, Norma and Beatrice. They lived on a farm in Plainfield, Wisconsin. Mabel's husband Oscar passed away in 1946. Oscar and Mabel are buried together in Plainfield Cemetery.

Ed Gein admitted he felt guilty about taking Mabel's body and ended up returning parts of Mrs. Everson to the grave site. He did, however, leave the body parts just below the surface of the ground. Mabel was originally buried in a wooden casket.

Eleanor M. Adams

Eleanor Adams was the fifth body Ed Gein dug up. Eleanor Adams was born Sunday, November 27, 1998 and passed away Monday, August 26, 1951. She was 52 years old.

Eleanor's husband Floyd was present when they exhumed Eleanor's casket. Also present were Sheriff Art Schley, Deputy Arnie Fritz, Plainfield village president, Harold Collins and 2 representatives from the Wisconsin State Crime Lab.

When they opened the casket, Eleanor's body was missing. Eleanor's plot was adjacent to Ed Gein's mother Augusta. Ed later confessed he dug up Eleanor's body the same day she was buried.

Eleanor's husband Floyd Adams later filed a $5,000 claim against the Gein Estate claiming mental suffering. Floyd and Eleanor had two children, a son, Floyd and a daughter, Barbara Jean.

Ursula Jane Callanan

Ursula Jane Callanan was the sixth body that Ed Gein dug up. Ursula was born Friday, January 14, 1877 and passed away on Saturday, November 29, 1952 in Los Angeles, California. She is buried in Plainfield Cemetery. Ursula was married to her husband Leroy and they had 4 children, three boys and one daughter. Leroy was born Monday, August 2, 1876 and passed away Sunday, November 29, 1931. Not a lot is known about Ursula Jane Callanan.

Ursula Jane Calanan

Lola E Foster

Lola Estelle Foster was the seventh body Ed Gein dug up. Lola was born on Monday, September 12, 1887 and passed away on Tuesday, February 17, 1953 at the age of 65. She was married to her husband Charles who was born Tuesday, September 6, 1887 and passed away Saturday, July 10, 1965. They lived on a farm in Hancock, Wisconsin. Charles and Lola had seven children, four boys, Norris, Elvin, Charles and Alan, along with three daughters: Marjorie, Emma and Marion. She is buried at Hancock Cemetery in Hancock, Wisconsin.

Lola Estelle Foster   Charles Foster   Lola and Charles Foster

Harriet Arabella Sherman

Harriett Sherman was the eighth body that Ed Gein dug up. Harriet was born Monday, May 4, 1885. She and her husband Edison had ten kids, six daughters named Edith, Marilla, Clara, Nora, Iva and Dorothy, along with four sons: Henry, Hugh, Raleigh and Sylvester. Edison was born Thursday, February 9, 1882 and passed away Tuesday, November 10, 1964. Edison was employed as a truck driver in the farming industry and Harriett was a housekeeper.

Harriett passed away Tuesday November 22nd, 1955 at the age of 70. Not a lot is known about Harriet's life. She was buried at the Plainfield Cemetery at N6590 Fifth Ave in Plainfield, Wisconsin.

Alzaida B. Abbott

Alzaida B. Abbot was the ninth body that Ed Gein dug up. Alzaida Abbott was born Saturday, March 3, 1883. Alzaida was employed as a nurse at the Madison Sanitariums located at the intersection of 404 N. Carroll Street and 114 E. Johnson Street in Madison, Wisconsin. She had one brother Herman and three sisters, Rosa, Cathie and Gladys. She lived at 1044 Spaight Street in Madison, Wisconsin. Alzaida Abbott passed away Wednesday, November 28, 1956 at the age of 72. She is buried in the Spirit Land Cemetery.

Alzaida B. Abbot

Chapter 3

Murdered Victims

Mary Hogan

Mary Hogan was born Mary Curran in 1901 in Duesenberg, Germany, to Frank and Antonia Curran. It is unknown when Mary came to the United States.

Mary married Joseph C. Hogan on October 4, 1920 in Springfield, Illinois. She divorced Joseph on December 23, 1925.

Mary married for a second time to Louis Peck on February 17, 1935 and divorced him on October 27, 1939.

Mary had a daughter, Christine Medved Selvo in 1927 who was raised in foster care. Mary worked in the composing room of the Chicago Carton Company located at 4200 Pulaski Road in Chicago from 1920-1946. She also worked as a die cut press feeder at Atlas Box Makers at 5025 W. 65th St. in Chicago from 1946-1948. During this time, Mary Hogan lived at 525 Leamington Street in Chicago. Mary moved to Babcock, Wisconsin in 1949 and bought The Fox Head Bar located at 140 Highway D in Babcock, Wisconsin.

Ed Gein frequented Mary's bar and on December 8, 1954 walked into The Fox Head Bar after closing and shot Mary with a .32 caliber pistol taking her life. He loaded Mary into his pickup and took her back to his place. Later that morning, Seymour Lester discovered blood at The Fox Head Bar and called the police. Police never found Mary Hogan until after they searched Ed Gein's farmhouse and found a skin face mask made from Mary Hogan's face.

Mary Hogan

525 Leamington Street Home in Chicago, IL

Atlas Box Makers
5025 W. 65th St, Chicago, IL

Chicago Carton Company
4200 Pulaski Rd, Chicago, IL

The Fox Head Bar

Current photo of the corner of Hwy D and Elm Rd where The Fox Head Bar was located.

Bernice C. Worden

Bernice Worden was born Bernice Conover on Monday, May 9, 1899 in Canton, Illinois to Frank and Angus Conover.

Bernice's father was part owner of the Worden Hardware Store with partner Leon Worden, Bernice's future husband. Bernice had three brothers Lester, Burl, Lloyd and one sister, Gladys.

Bernice and Leon took over the Worden Hardware Store located at 110 S. Main Street in 1931. Prior to being a hardware store, the building used to be Schultz Garage.

Leon and Bernice had one son, Frank Worden, who was born on Monday, November 27, 1922. Frank later lived at 226 Poplar Street in Plainfield, Wisconsin.

Leon Worden passed away on Sunday, February 15, 1931 at the age of 40 leaving Bernice to run the store alone. Bernice was a member of the American Legion Auxiliary of Plainfield and was a member of the Grand Chapter of the Wisconsin Order of the Eastern Star out of Wautoma, Wisconsin.

On the morning of November 16, 1957 at around 8:00 am, Ed Gein came into the Worden Hardware Store for some antifreeze. He took the antifreeze out to his car. He returned to the store and asked Bernice if he could see the .22 caliber rifle in the rack. Bernice handed the rifle to Ed and she went to look out the window viewing the Shell Station located across the street. Ed pulled a .22 caliber shell out of his pocket, loaded it into the rifle, pointed the rifle at Bernice and shot her in the back of the head, killing her. Bernice fell to the ground and Ed dragged Bernice's body to the rear of the store and onto the loading dock. He placed her body into the back of the Worden Hardware delivery pick up and drove it to East Road where he parked it in the pine trees. Ed walked back to the hardware store, where his car was parked. Then Ed drove his car out to East Road where the Worden's truck was parked. He then loaded Bernice Worden's lifeless body into his trunk and drove home.

Frank Worden came back from hunting and when he walked into the store, he noticed a pool of blood on the floor. He saw on the store sales register that Ed Gein had bought antifreeze earlier in the day. Frank informed the police. Bernice's body was found at 2:00 pm that same day hanging from the rafters at Ed Gein's farm. Bernice Worden was killed by Ed Gein on Saturday, November 16th, 1957 at 8:00 am, she was 58 years old.

Worden Hardware Store was originally Paul's Garage

Bernice Worden   Bernice Worden's Home

The truck Ed Gein used to haul Bernice Worden's body to his car.

The **hearse bearing Bernice Worden's casket drives past her hardware store on the morning of her funeral.** (Wide World)

Bernice Worden Funeral   Bernice's Funeral at United Methodist Church

Worden Hardware Store building in 2021

Chapter 4

Other Investigations

Georgia Jean Weckler

Eight-year old Georgia Jean Weckler was born on June 27, 1938 and disappeared on May 1, 1947 between 3:15 & 3:30 pm from her Fort Atkinson, Wisconsin home. She was abducted at the end of her driveway on the corner of Highway 12 & County J.

This case has remained unresolved. Ed Gein was given a lie detector test and passed, so he was not a suspect. A black 1935 black Ford car was seen near the scene. Buford Sennett admitted to taking and killing Georgia Winkler before his death in 2002. No proof was ever found that he committed this crime.

Georgia Jean Weckler

Victor Travis & Ray Burgess

On November 1, 1952, Victor Travis, age 43, of Plainfield, Wisconsin and Ray Burgess of Milwaukee disappeared after a long day of drinking at Mac's Bar in Plainfield.

No trace of these two hunters was ever found. When Ed Gein was questioned about these two disappearances, Ed denied having anything to do with it.

Young Victor Travis

Evelyn Hartley

Evelyn Hartley, age 15, disappeared on Saturday, October 24, 1953. Ed Gein was questioned if he had anything to do with the disappearance of Evelyn Hartley. Ed Gein was allegedly in La Crosse, Wisconsin at his cousin Clem's home that was located two blocks away at the time Evelyn Hartley went missing.

Evelyn was born Sunday, November 21, 1937 and lived with her parents at 1533 Johnson St in La Crosse, Wisconsin. Her body has never been discovered so there is no proof of the date of her death. Evelyn was a sophomore at Central High School. Her father, Richard Hartley, was a biology professor at La Crosse State College and her mother, Ethel was a home maker.

Evelyn disappeared while babysitting for Professor Viggo Rasmussen at his home located at 2415 Hoeschler Drive in La Crosse. Police claim a basement window was broken into and there were blood spots in the basement. Evelyn was wearing red jeans, a white blouse, glasses and bobby socks.

Ed Gein was given two lie detector tests about Evelyn Hartley and he passed both so he was no longer a suspect. To this day, the case of Evelyn Hartley has never been solved. Ed did have relatives by the name of Gus and Augusta Larky, who lived in La Crosse, just a short distance from where Evelyn Hartley was taken. He also had a Cousin Clem that he visited in La Crosse as well.

Evelyn Hartley

Evelyn Harley's Home

Prof. Viggo Rasmussen Home

Chapter 5

Gein Family Timeline

Gein Family Timeline

1873   Ed's father George "Gee" was born. George later changed his last name to "Gein".

1878   Ed's mother Augusta Wilhelmine was born.

1902   Ed's brother Henry Gein was born on January 17.

1906   Ed Gein was born to George and Augusta Gein at their home at 612 Gould Street in La Crosse, Wisconsin.

1906   Henry Gein was 5 years old.

1906   Augusta opens A. Gein Mercantile at 914 Caledonia Street in La Crosse, Wisconsin.

1913   Ed (age 7) witnesses his parents slaughter a hog in the shed behind the store.

1913   The Gein's move to Camp Douglas, Wisconsin.

1914   Augusta moves the family to Plainfield, Wisconsin, to a 195-acre farm because she wanted to move away from the immorality of the city and the sinners that inhabited it. Ed was 8 years old.

1914   Ed and Henry began school in Roche-a-Cri Grade School. A tiny one-room building with 12 students. Ed was 8 years old.

1920   Ed graduated from eighth grade and dropped out of school. Ed was 14 years old.

1940   Ed's father George Gein dies April 1 of pneumonic fluid in the lungs at the age of 66. Ed was 34 years old and Henry was 39 years old. Both brothers took on odd jobs to help support the family.

1942   Ed was eligible for the draft and had to travel to Milwaukee, Wisconsin for a physical exam. He was rejected due to a growth in his left eyelid, which slightly impaired his vision. Henry was also rejected because of his age.

1944   On May 16 Henry died a sudden death under mysterious circumstances, at the age of 43. Ed and Henry were fighting a brushfire on Henry's land. Ed reported that he was unable to locate Henry, but then led police directly to where he lay, dead. Apparent cause of death was not consistent with injuries from the fire. Henry's body was untouched by the fire but had an apparent bump on his head. Ed is 38 years old and had his mother all to himself.

1944   On May 18 the County Corner listed Henry's cause of death as asphyxiation. The police dismissed the notion of foul play.

1944   Augusta suffers her first stroke in late 1944.

1945   On December 29 Augusta dies of complications from a second stroke at the age of 67. Ed reacts by boarding up his mother's bedroom and sitting room trying to preserve them as if she were still alive. Ed was 39 years old.

1946   Ed continues to live on the farm and live off meager earnings from the odd jobs he did around town and babysitting. He rented out sections of land for which people would not pay him. Ed was 40 years old.

1947	February, eighteen months after Augusta dies, Ed, driven by intense loneliness and what he later said to have strange visions, began to think he could raise the dead by his own will. Ed went to Spirit Land Cemetery and dug up his first victim, Grace Beggs. Ed later said he scouted the obituaries for potential bodies that reminded him of his mother. Ed did say he tried to dig up his mother, but the soil was too sandy. Ed was 41 years old.
1947	On May 1, 8-year-old Georgia Jean Weckler disappeared without a trace, leaving no suspects. The only clue found was a tire track from a Ford. She was taken at the end of her driveway after school in Fort Atkinson, WI.
1950	Ed goes to Plainfield Cemetery and digs up his second body: Elise Sparks. This would have been at the end of March or the beginning of April. Ed was 43 years old.
1951	Ed goes back to Plainfield Cemetery and digs up his third body: Marie Bergstrom. Ed would have taken her after February 6.
1951	Ed digs up his fourth body from the Plainfield Cemetery sometime after May 15: Mabel Everson.
1951	Ed digs up his fifth body Eleanor Adams from the Plainfield Cemetery. This would occur after August 26. Ed was 45 years old.
1952	Victor Travis, age 42, and friend Ray Burgess disappear after spending several hours at a local bar in Plainfield. No trace of them or their car was ever found.

1952	Ed digs up his sixth body from the Plainfield Cemetery. Ursula Jane Calanan was taken by Ed after November 29. Ed was 46 years old.
1953	On October 24, Evelyn Hartley age 15 is abducted while babysitting for friends at 2415 Hoeshier Street in La Crosse, Wisconsin. Her body was never found. Ed was 47 years old.
1953	Ed digs up his seventh body, Lola Foster from Hancock Wisconsin Cemetery. Ed was 48 years old.
1954	On December 8, Mary Hogan disappears from her bar in Babcock, The Fox Head Bar. Ed killed her with a .22 caliber pistol.
1957	On November 16, Bernice Worden age 58 disappeared from her hardware store. Her son, Deputy Frank Worden returned from deer hunting to find his mother gone. Sheriff Arthur Schley responded to Frank Worden's call. Upon entering the store, he noticed blood on the floor and a .22 caliber rifle that was out of place on its rack at the store. In the receipt book, they noticed that Ed Gein had bought antifreeze earlier in the day. Sheriff Schley and a deputy went to Ed Gein's farm and found Bernice Worden's body hung by the rafters, gutted like a deer.
1957	On November 17, Ed Gein was taken into custody at the home of Lester Hill at N6520 3rd Street. Ed was enjoying a pork chop dinner before he was arrested in the Hill's driveway.
1957	On November 18th Ed Gein confesses to killing Mary Hogan and Bernice Worden. An autopsy report reveals Mrs. Worden died of a single gunshot wound to the back of the

head. Ed was 51 years old. Ed was arrested by Deputy Dan Chase.

| 1957 | On November 22nd, Ed was taken before Judge Boyd Clark charged with robbery. The murder charge was held back in order to determine his sanity. |

1957 On November 22nd, Ed was taken before Judge Boyd Clark charged with robbery. The murder charge was held back in order to determine his sanity.

1957 On November 23rd, the psychologist and psychiatrist who interviewed Ed asserted that he was schizophrenic.

1957 On November 24, the graves of Eleanor Adams and Marie Bergstrom were exhumed and found empty.

1957 On November 29, deputies found more bones buried in a trench on Ed's farm.

1957 On December 17, the judge received a packet from the Central State Hospital stating that Ed was insane and should be permanently committed to the hospital.

1958 On January 6, Ed has a sanity hearing in Wisconsin Rapids. He was declared legally insane by Judge Herbert Bunde and he was recommitted to Central State Hospital.

1958 On January 22 at 1:00 pm Ed's trial begins in Wautoma.

1958 On March 20, Ed's farm was burned to the ground by a mysterious fire.

1958 On March 30 anything left after the fire was auctioned off. Ed was 52 years old.

1962 All body remains found on Ed Gein's property were returned from Madison State Crime Lab to Plainfield to be buried in a mass unmarked grave.

1968	On January 22, after spending ten years in an institution, Ed was determined to be competent to stand trial and the proceedings began. It took 9 months to pass the preliminary matters such as evidence, filing for briefs and appointment of counsel.
1968	On November 7, the actual trial begins.
1968	On November 14th, Ed Gein was found guilty of first degree murder for the shooting of Bernice Worden, but the court also found that on the day of the shooting, Ed was not insane. Ed was returned to Central State Hospital. Ed was 62 years old.
1968	On March 22nd Sheriff Arthur Schley, the arresting officer, dies of a heart attack at age 60.
1974	Ed filed a petition with the Waushara County Clerk of Courts claiming that he has now recovered from his mental illness, is fully competent and wants to be released.
1974	On June 27, a judge reviewed Ed's petition and ordered a re-examination. The judge rejected Ed's petition and he was returned to the hospital. Ed was 68 years old.
1978	Ed was moved to the Mendota Mental Institute in Madison. Ed was 72 years old.
1984	On July 26, Ed was senile and after a long battle with cancer, died of respiratory failure in the geriatric ward at Mendota. Ed was 78 years old.
1984	On July 27, at 4:00 pm Ed Gein was buried by Bennie P. and Betty J. Petrusky in a blue casket, between his mother and brother.

Chapter 6

Photo Library

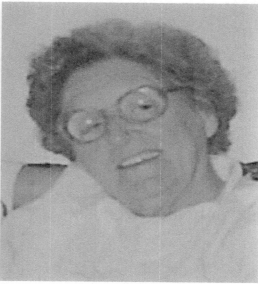

Bernice Worden

Worden Hardware Store in Plainfield, Wisconsin

Main Street in Plainfield, Wisconsin

Worden Hardware Store

Paul Reindfliesch Ford Garage, Corner of Main Street & North Street   Plainfield, WI

The Ford Garage before it was Worden's Hardware Store

Worden's Hardware Store in 1958

Mrs. Worden's Home...

This is the modest home of Mrs. Worden in Plainfield. She lived in the home alone, six blocks from the hardware store she operated.

Bernice Worden's funeral

Bernice Worden being carried out after the funeral

Bernice Worden's last ride past the Worden Hardware Store and on the way to the Plainfield Cemetery

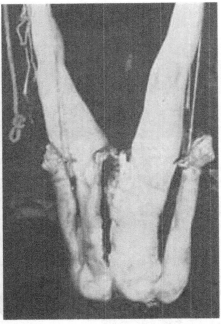

Frank Worden on the left

Bernice Worden's body as it was found at Ed Gein's farm

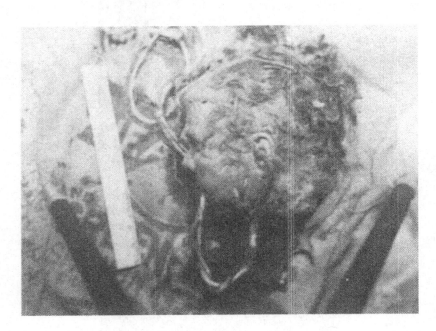

Bernice Worden's head

Bernice Worden's head

District Attorney Earl Kileen

Elmo Ueek (Ed used to work for him.)

Lester Hill

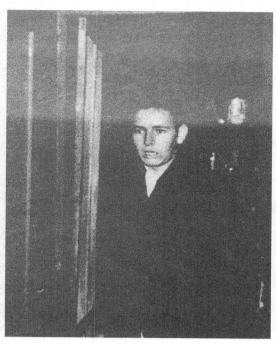

Mrs. Clifford Banks. Ed babysat her children.

Robert Hill

Ed's mother Augusta Gein

George and Augusta Gein

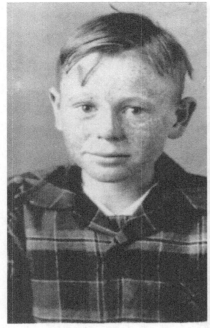 

Young Ed Gein   Ed Gein

Ed Gein   Ed Gein with Sheriff Art Schley

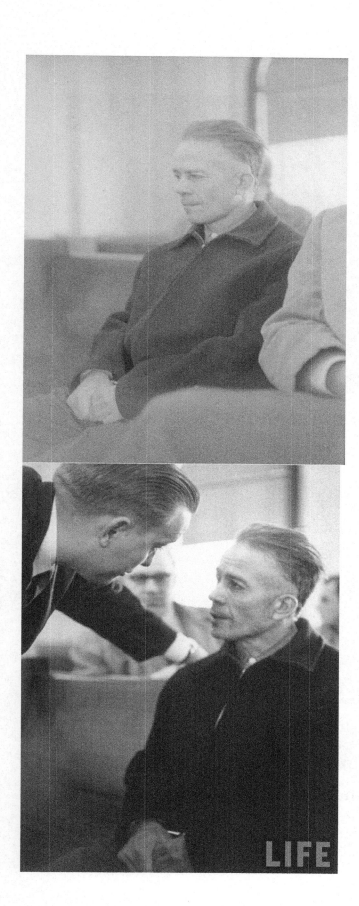

Ed Gein in court

Ed in court alongside Sheriff Art Schley

Ed right next to Sheriff Art Schley

Ed Gein at the state crime lab with Sheriff Schley

Ed in court   Ed Gein and Sheriff Arthur Schley

Ed Gein outside the Waushara County Jail

Older Ed Gein

Ed Gein in court

Ed Gein outside the Waushara County Jail

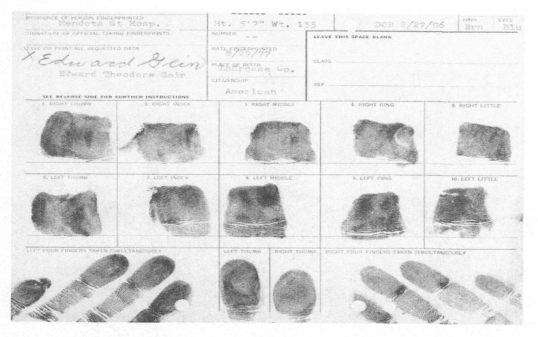

Ed Gein's fingerprints

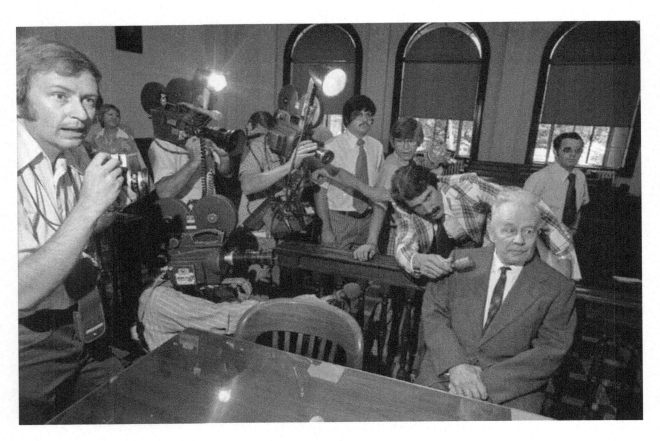

Ed Gein in court

The boarded up farm of Ed Gein

Gein farmhouse boarded up

Ed Gein's home shortly after his arrest

Ed Gein's home

Ed Gein with Sheriff Batterman   Ed Gein's skin chair

Waushara County Jail where Ed was held

Ed Gein's kitchen

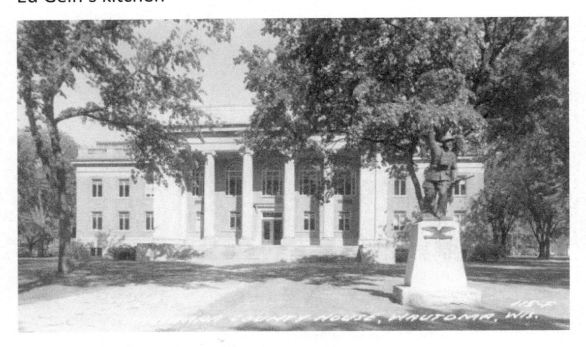

Waushara County Court House

Augusta Gein's bedroom

Curiosity seekers

Ed's violin

Unknown victim

Ed's bedroom

Robert Hill

Ed Gein's farm the day of the auction

Hill's driveway where Ed Gein was arrested

Auction advertisement

Day of auction

Aerial view of Ed Gein's farm

Gein home at 1032 St. Charles Street, La Crosse, Wisconsin

Ed Gein's birth house at 912 Gould Street, La Crosse, Wisconsin

Gein home at 1931 Wood Street, La Crosse, Wisconsin

Mary Hogan   Older Mary Hogan

Mary Hogan's Fox Head Bar. She lived in the rear of the building.

1957 Outside the Waushara Jail

Same location in 2021

1974 Outside the Waushara Jail

Same location in 2021

Unknown date Outside the Waushara Jail

Same location in 2021

1957 Ed Gein in squad car

Same location in 2021 at the old Waushara Jail.

Unknown date

Same location in 2021

Mrs. Worden's Home . . .

This is the modest home of Mrs. Worden in Plainfield. She lived in the home alone, six blocks from the hardware store she operated.

1957

Same location in 2021

1954 Mary Hogan's Fox Head Bar.

Same location in 2021

1957

Same location in 2021

Unknown date Outside the Waushara Jail.

Same location in 2021

1957 Bernice Worden's funeral

Same location in 2021

Chapter 7

Court Records

STATE OF WISCONSIN   CIRCUIT COURT   WAUSHARA COUNTY

— —

STATE OF WISCONSIN,

                 Plaintiff,

vs.

EDWARD GEIN,

         Defendant.

BRIEF IN OPPOSITION
TO DEFENDANT'S
MOTION TO SUPPRESS
EVIDENCE

— —

QUESTION

Did the discovery of the body of the victim and the cash register on the premises of the defendant comport with the requirements of the Fourth Amendment of the United States constitution and Article I, Section II of the Wisconsin constitution?

FACTS

Around supper time on the 16th of November, 1957 law enforcement authorities in Waushara County, Wisconsin were apprised concerning circumstances at the Worden Hardware Store in the town of Plainfield indicating that Mrs. Bernice Worden, the operator of the store, had met with foul play. Specifically, they were advised that Mrs. Worden, who should have been on the premises, was not, and a pool of blood was observed in the Worden Hardware Store and "a kind of trail of it led into the back room" of the store. (Testimony of Leon Murty, Deputy Sheriff of Waushara County in 1957 as reflected at page 27 of the transcript at the hearing conducted on April 24, 1968 -- all page references hereinafter made are to said transcript). The blood was on the floor, "and there was some kind of skid marks like something had been moved through it or dragged through it ... Well it

looked to me like the heels of a person's shoes". (Pages 34-35).
From other information obtained from Mrs. Worden's son, Frank,
and other persons at the scene, the investigating authorities
concluded that Mr. Edward Gein was apparently involved (Pages
38, 39, 40 and Pages 88 and 89 -- this last from the testimony
of Lloyd Shoephoester, County Police, Green Lake, Wisconsin).
This information was to the effect that Mr. Gein had the day
before asked Mrs. Worden to go roller skating, had inquired
whether Frank Worden intended to go deer hunting on November 16,
had been advised that Frank was going hunting, and had advised
Frank and Mrs. Worden that he, Mr. Gein, would return the following day to purchase some antifreeze; that in fact a slip on a
peg in the store indicated that someone had purchased antifreeze
on November 16, and that Mr. Gein had been observed operating
the Worden truck during the afternoon of November 16, 1957.
Based upon that information County Police Officer, Lloyd Shoephoester
and Sheriff Art Schley of Waushara County proceeded to Ed Gein's
farm at 7:30 P.M. on November 16, 1957. According to the testimony
of Officer Shoephoester "we went out there because from the
evidence we had we believed that she (Mrs. Worden) might be at
the Gein farm". They didn't know whether ornot she was dead or
alive but felt that in all probability she was injured; they
felt there was an emergency situation and they were interested
in finding Mrs. Worden. (Pages 88-90 of the transcript). On
arriving at the Gein farm Officer Shoephoester entered through a
closed but unlocked door to a woodshed connected to and at the
back of the Gein residence. Inside the woodshed Officer Shoephoester

-2-

and Sheriff Schley discovered the body of Mrs. Worden and the cash register which had been removed from the store.

ARGUMENT

At the time Officer Shoephoester and Sheriff Schley entered the woodshed they did not have a warrant to search the premises of Mr. Gein, they did not have consent of Mr. Gein to search his premises and they were not searching the premises of Mr. Gein incident to an arrest.

Two questions are raised in this case. First, was the entry and the consequent discovery by the officers a "search and seizure" and therefore subject to the constitutional provisions of both the United States and Wisconsin constitutions? Second, if the entry and observation of the body is properly denominated a "search and seizure" was it lawful?

Officer Shoephoester clearly indicated that after the officers entry into the shed it did not require a "search" in the traditional use of the word, to find Mrs. Worden's body. (Transcript Page 94). It required no rummaging about among the effects of the defendant to discover the body. See dissenting opinion of Justice Douglas in Warden v. Hayden (1967) 387 U.S. 294, 87 S. ct. 1642, 18 L. ed 2d 782, at page 800 (all page references made in citing United States Supreme Court decisions in this brief will be to Lawyers Edition citation).

It is submitted that the question of whether or not the mere observations of persons are properly denominated a search has never been specifically resolved by the United States Supreme Court. Indeed there is a theory that even where there is a

-3-

trespass the Fourth Amendment does not automatically apply to
evidence obtained by sound or sight. See dissenting opinion of
Justice Black in Katz v. United States (1967) 389 U.S. 347,
88 S. Ct. 507, 19 L. ed 2d 576 at page 592. This theory,
however, depends upon arguing the continuing vitality of Olmstead
v. United States (1928) 277 U.S. 438, 48 S. Ct. 564, 72 L. ed 934
and Hester v. United States (1924) 265 U.S. 57, 44 S. Ct. 445,
68 L. ed 898. To quote Olmstead at page 951:

> "Justice Bradley in the Boyd case and Justice
> Clarke in the Gouled case, said that the Fifth
> Amendment and the Fourth Amendment would be
> liberally construed to affect the purpose of the
> framers of the constitution inthe interests of
> liberty. But that cannot justify enlargement
> of the language employed beyond the possible
> practical meaning of houses, persons, papers,
> and effects, OR SO TO APPLY THE WORDS 'SEARCH
> AND SEIZURE' AS TO FORBID HEARING OR SIGHT."
> (emphasis supplied)

However, the continuing vitality of Olmstead is doubtful
in light of the majority opinion in Katz.

Although in State v. Hoyt (1964) 21 Wis 2d 310, 317u
the Wisconsin Supreme Court had appeared to conclude that visual
observations of evidence in full view was not a search:

> "The United States Supreme Court has held that
> evidence in the full view of a police officer appear-
> ing on the scene, and subsequently taken into custody
> by him, is not brought into his control by means of
> a search (citing United States v. Rabinowitz (1950)
> 339 U.S. 56, 70 S. Ct. 430, 94 L. ed 653).
> We conclude that because the officers were justified
> in their original entry into the Hoyt living room
> and because the bringing of the gun into their
> custody was not the consequence of a search, the
> Fourth Amendment, binding upon the states through
> the due-process clause of the Fourteenth Amendment
> was not violated."

However, in the Hoyt rehearing opinion at 21 Wis 2d 284
and more forcefully in Edwards v. State (1968) 38 Wis 2d 332 at

-4-

page 338 the court appeared to significantly modify its position:

> "A search can be conducted by ones eyes alone.
> However, 'a search implies a prying into hidden
> places for that which is concealed'. It is not
> a search to observe what is in plain view. Even
> though visual surveillance of things within plain
> view may be regarded as a search the real issue
> to be settled is whether or not such activities
> are regarded as an unreasonable search as cir-
> sumscribed by either the Fourth Amendment of
> the United States constitution or Art. I, Sec. II
> of the Wisconsin constitution."

In Terry v. Ohio, the "stop and frisk" case decided by
the United States Supreme Court on June 10, 1968, 3 Cr. L. 3149,
Chief Justice Warren, speaking for the majority, supported the
Wisconsin position announced in Edwards at footnote 15, 3 Cr. L.
3154:

> "In our view the sounder course is to recognize
> that the Fourth Amendment governs all intrusions
> by agents of the public upon personal security,
> and to make the scope of the particular intrusion,
> in light of all the exigencies of the case, a
> central element in the analysis of reasonableness
> ... This seems preferable to an approach which
> attributes too much significance to an overly
> technical definition of 'search',"

In the case at bar, then, the entry and observation of
the officers can, in all probability be properly denominated a
"search and seizure" and the real question considered; what
the Wisconsin Supreme Court has aptly described as "the real
issue to be settled", to-wit: whether or not the search can
be sustained as resonable under the Fourth Amendment of the United
States constitution and Article I Section II of the Wisconsin
constitution. The State submits that it can be so sustained.

To crystalize the issue the State reiterates that at
the time Officer Shoephoester and Sheriff Schley entered the woodshed attached to Mr. Gein's house they did not have a warrant

-5-

to search his premises, and in fact no search warrant had been
or ever was obtained by anyone; they did not have consent from
Mr. Gein to search his premises, and their search was not
incident to any lawful arrest because at that time Mr. Gein
was being taken into custody by other police officers at a place
distant from his premises. Nonetheless, the State submits that
under the attendant circumstances then and there existent, the
search was reasonable under the Fourth Amendment of the United
States constitution and Article I, Section II of the Wisconsin
constitution.

In 1948 Justice Jackson writing for the United States
Supreme Court in Johnson v. United States 333 U.S. 10, 68 S. Ct.
367, 92 L. ed 436 declared at page 440-441:

> "There are exceptional circumstances in which,
> on balancing the need for effective law enforcement
> against the right of privacy, it may be contended
> that a magistrate's warrant for search may be
> dispensed with."

This doctrine known variously as the exigent circumstances
rule or the exceptional circumstances rule has been repeatedly
reaffirmed since that date and threads its way through all the
applicable search and seizure law of the United States Supreme
Court, and Wisconsin Supreme Court. It is upon this theory
that the State submits that the search in the instant case is
sustained under the Fourth Amendment to the United States
constitution, and Article I, Section II of the Wisconsin constitution.

A brief review of the doctrine up to and including the
most recent case law, is appropriate.

-6-

93

Later in 1948 the United States Supreme Court decided McDonald v. United States 355 U.S. 451, 69 S. Ct. 191, L. ed 153. It is of note that counsel for the defendant in his brief quotes extensively from and relies heavily upon McDonald (See pages 6 and 7 of Brief of the defendant). To quote the pertinent language of McDonald is to hoist the defendant on his own petard: At page 158:

> "Where, as here, officers are not responding to an emergency, there must be compelling reasons to justify the absence of a search warrant. A SEARCH WITHOUT A WARRANT DEMANDS EXCEPTIONAL CIRCUMSTANCES, AS WE HELD IN JOHNSON ..." (emphasis supplied)

And further:

> "... Absent some grave emergency, the Fourth Amendment has interposed a magistrate between the citizen and the police. This was done not to shield criminals nor to make the home a safe haven for illegal activities. It was done so that an objective mind might weigh the need to invade that privacy in order to enforce the law. The right of privacy was deemed too precious to entrust to the discretion of those whose job is the detection of crime and the arrest of criminals. Power is a heady thing; and history shows that the police acting on their own cannot be trusted. And so the constitution requires a magistrate to pass on the desires of the police before they violate the privacy of the home. We cannot be true to that constitutional requirement and excuse the absence of a search warrant WITHOUT A SHOWING BY THOSE WHO SEEK EXEMPTION FROM THE CONSTITUTIONAL MANDATE THAT THE EXIGENCIES OF THE SITUATION MADE THAT COURSE IMPERATIVE." (emphasis supplied)

Justice Jackson in his concurring opinion in McDonald declared at page 160:

> "Whether there is reasonable necessity for a search without waiting to obtain a warrant certainly depends somewhat upon the gravity of the offense thought to be in progress as well as the hazards of the method of attempting to reach it ... (The) criminal operation ... (in this case) ... was not one which endangered life or limb or the peace and good order of the community even if it continued another day or

-7-

two; ... It is to me a shocking proposition that private homes, ... may be indiscrimately invaded at the descretion of any suspicious police officer engaged in following up offenses THAT INVOLVE NO VIOLENCE OR THREATS OF IT. While I should be human enough to apply the letter of the law with some indulgence to officers acting to deal with threats of crimes of violence which endanger life or security, it is notable that few of the searches found by this court to be unlawful dealt with that catagory of crime. Almost without exception the overzeal was in suppressing acts not malum in se but only malum prohibitum". (emphasis supplied)

At that juncture in this opinion, Justice Jackson inserted a footnote in which he gives as examples the nature of the crimes involved in search cases which had theretofore been brought to the attention of the United States Supreme Court. He then went on:

"While the enterprise of parting fools from their money by their 'numbers' lottery is one that ought to be suppressed, I do not think its suppression is more important to society than the security of the people against unreasonable searches and seizures. WHEN AN OFFICER UNDERTAKES TO ACT AS HIS OWN MAGISTRATE, HE OUGHT TO BE IN A POSITION TO JUSTIFY IT BY POINTING TO SOME REAL IMMEDIATE AND SERIOUS CONSEQUENCES IF HE POSPONED ACTION TO GET A WARRANT" (emphasis supplied)

The significance of the McDonald decision as it relates to the case at bar is of course that it clearly recognizes that there are exceptional circumstances which dictate swift police action and obviate the necessity of appearance before a magistrate to obtain a search warrant. As Justice Jackson indicated these circumstances arise and can be justified usually where the crime is one involving violence or the possibility of harm to the officers or to others and the attendant circumstances are such that immediate action is required. Further, the State is obligated

-8-

to demonstrate these exigent circumstances to the trial court. It is submitted that in the case at bar this is exactly the situation that met the law enforcement officers in Waushara County on November 16, 1957. A crime of violence had obviously been committed and the victim of that violence, her condition unknown, was in all probability to be found on the premises of the defendant. Under those circumstances and in that situation the course that the officers took was in the language of McDonald "imperative"; and the "grave emergency" required to justify such action was obvious and required urgent response by the authorities.

The Wisconsin Supreme Court acknowledged the exigent circumstances rule in 1964 in State v. Hoyt, 21 Wis 2d 284, rehearing at page 296:

> "The Fourth amendment to the constitution of the United States and sec. 11, art. 1 of the constitution of Wisconsin guarantee security of houses 'against unreasonable searches and seizures.' The officers had received information of a shooting at this address. They were able to see a body on the floor within. No one answered their rings. Under these circumstances it was their duty to enter at least for the purpose of determining whether the body was alive or dead, and to render assistance if alive.
>
> It has been recognized, sometimes in dictum, that emergency situations may present compelling reasons for an immediate search without warrant, which may nevertheless be reasonable. A search incident to arrest is the most commonly recognized instance of a reasonable search without a search warrant.
>
> In the instant case the purpose of assisting the victim if still alive supplied a compelling reason for immediate entry, quite apart from the purpose of prosecuting for crime. In civil cases where a fireman or policeman attempts recovery for being injured upon private property in the course of performing a duty, he is held not to be a trespasser. Where a conflagration is raging, a person may lawfully enter upon another premises in order to save others, and he is not regarded as a trespasser. In other situations necessity, especially in the interest of preservation of human life, will legally excuse or justify trespass.

-9-

We conclude that in the present case the officers lawfully entered the home and their observations incidental to lawful entry did not constitute an unreasonable search."

A rash of recent cases in the United States Supreme Court have reiterated the rule. In Warden v. Hayden 387 U.S. 294, 37 S. Ct. 1642 L. ed 2d 782, at page 787 the court declared:

"... neither the entry without warrant to search for the robber, nor the search for him without warrant was invalid. UNDER THE CIRCUMSTANCES OF THIS CASE 'THE EXIGENCIES OF THE SITUATION MADE THAT COURSE IMPERATIVE'. (citing McDonald)" (emphasis supplied)

And further:

"The Fourth Amendment does not require police officers to delay the course of an investigation if to do so would gravely endanger their lives OR THE LIVES OF OTHERS. Speed here was essential ..." (emphasis supplied)

The above quotation is cited with approval in Katz v. United States (1967) 389 U.S. 347, 88 S. Ct. 507, 19 L. ed 2d 576 at page 586, footnote 21 and Justice Harlen in his concurring opinion in Katz at page 588 declared:

"As elsewhere under the Fourth Amendment, warrants are the general rule, to which the legitimate needs of the law enforcement may demand specific exceptions."

And finally in Katz, Justice White in his concurring opinion at page 589 stated:

"In joining the court's opinion, I note the court's acknowledgement that there are circumstances in which it is reasonable to search without a warrant."

In Terry v. Ohio decided June 10, 1968, 3CrL 3149 Chief Justice Warren speaking for the majority at page 3151:

"Of course, the specific content and incidents of this right (Fourth Amendment protection) must be shaped by the context in which it is asserted. For 'what the constitution forbids is not all searches and seizures, but unreasonable searches and seizures' Elkins v. United States, 364 U.S. 206, 222 (1960)."

-10-

At pages 3154-3155:

"The scope of the search must be 'strictly tied to
and justified by' the circumstances which rendered
its initiation permissible. Warden v. Hayden, 387
U.S. 294, 310 (1967) (Mr. Justice Fortas, concurring)
..... the central inquiry under the Fourth Amendment --
the reasonableness in all the circumstances of the
particular governmental invasion of a citizen's
personal security. .....We must decide whether at
that point it was reasonable for Officer McFadden to
have interfered with petitioner's personal security as
he did. And in determining whether the seizure and
search were 'unreasonable' our inquiry is a dual one --
whether the officer's action was justified at its
inception, and whether it was reasonably related in
scope TO THE CIRCUMSTANCES WHICH JUSTIFIED THE INTER-
FERENCE IN THE FIRST PLACE. ..... in most instances
failure to comply with the warrant requirement can
only be excused by exigent circumstances, ...In order
to assess the reasonableness of Officer McFadden's
conduct as a general proposition, it is necessary
'first to focus upon the governmental interest which
allegedly justified official intrusion upon the
constitutionally protected interests of the private
citizen,' for there is 'no ready test for determining
reasonableness other than by balancing the need to
search (or seize) against the invasion which the
search (or seizure) entails.' Camara v. Municipal
Court, 387 U.S. 523, 534, 536-537 (1967). AND IN
JUSTIFYING THE PARTICULAR INTRUSION THE POLICE OFFICER
MUST BE ABLE TO POINT TO SPECIFIC AND ARTICULABLE
FACTS WHICH, TAKEN TOGETHER WITH RATIONAL INFERENCES
FROM THOSE FACTS, REASONABLY WARRANT THAT INTRUSION.[18]

(Footnote 18 - This demand for specificity in the
information upon which police action is predicated is
the central teaching of this Court's Fourth Amendment
jurisprudence. See Beck v. Ohio, 379 U.S. 89, 96-97
(1964); Ker v. California, 374 U.S. 23, 34-47 (1963);
Wong Sun v. United States, 371 U.S. 471, 479-484 (1963);
Rios v. United States, 364 U.S. 253, 261-262 (1960);
Henry v. United States, 361 U.S. 98, 100-102 (1959);
Draper v. United States, 358 U.S. 307, 312-314 (1959);
Brinegar v. United States, 338 U.S. 160, 175-178
(1949); Johnson v. United States, 333 U.S. 10, 15-17
(1948); United States v. Di Re, 332 U.S. 581, 593-595
(1948); Husty v. United States, 282 U.S. 694, 700-701
(1931); Dumbra v. United States, 268 U.S. 435, 441
(1925); Carroll v. United States, 267 U.S. 132, 159-
162 (1925); Stacey v. Emery, 97 U.S. 642, 645 (1878).

-11-

...WOULD THE FACTS AVAILABLE TO THE OFFICER AT THE
MOMENT OF THE SEIZURE OR THE SEARCH 'WARRANT A MAN
OF REASONABLE CAUTION IN THE BELIEF' THAT THE ACTION
TAKEN WAS APPROPRIATE? Cf. Carroll v. United States
267 U.S. 132 (1925); Beck v. Ohio, 379 U.S. 89, 96-97
(1964)." (emphasis supplied)

At page 3156-3157:

"...A search for weapons inthe absence of probable
cause to arrest, however, must, like any other search,
be strictly circumscribed by the exigencies which
justify its initiation. Warden v. Hayden, 387 U.S.
294, 310 (1967) (Mr. Justice Fortas, concurring).
.....The officer need not be absolutely certain that
the individual is armed; the issue is whether a
reasonably prudent man in the circumstances would be
warranted in the belief that his safety or that of
others was in danger. Cf. Beck v. Ohio, 379 U.S. 89,
91 (1964); Brinegar v. United States, 388 U.S. 160,
174-176 (1949); Stacey v. Emery, 97 U.S. 642, 645
(1878). And in determining whether the officer acted
reasonably in such circumstances, due weight must be
given, not to his inchoate and unparticularized suspicion or 'hunch', but to the specific reasonable
inferences which he is entitled to draw from the facts
in light of his experience. Cf. Brinegar v. United
States supra."

In the companion case to Terry v. Ohio, Sibron v. New York

3 CrL 3160 at page 3165:

"...The constitutional validity of a warrantless
search is pre-eminently the sort of question which
can only be decided in the concrete factual context
of the individual case."

and Justice Harlan concurring at page 3169:

"While no hard-and-fast rule can be drawn, I would
suggest that one important factor, missing here, that
should be taken into account in determining whether
there are reasonable grounds for a forcible intrusion
is whether there is any need for immediate action."

It can be seen then that the Supreme Court of the United
States has scrupulously carved out an area of reasonable
warrantless searches which do no violence to the Fourth Amendment.
Admittedly, these situations are rare and defined always by the
circumstances in which they are found. However, the search in

-12-

the instant case is one of those reasonable under the exigent circumstances doctrine. Applying the applicable case law leads to the inescapable conclusion that the search was lawful and reasonable under the Fourth Amendment of the United States constitution.

As Justice Wilkie succinctly put it in Edwards v. State, (1968) 38 Wis. 2d 332 at page 340:

> "... the test to be applied in determining whether a search is constitutional is one of reasonableness under the circumstances."

In determining whether emergency conditions justified the action taken and thus cloaked the search with the concomitant reasonableness necessary for it to fall within the ambit of searches sanctioned under the applicable Fourth Amendment standards, the setting and circumstances of the search must be closely scrutinized and all of the factors pertinent considered.

The state submits that such scrutiny in the case at bar vindicates the search as the only "common sense" reasonable approach under the circumstances. Legal debate before a magistrate would have consumed "precious time" and would have been foolish. It must be remembered that the object of the inquiry here was not narcotics, distilled spirits, contraband or tools for committing crime, but was rather a human being. Defendant's counsel in his brief accurately points out that the fruits of a search cannot be used to vindicate it. Nonetheless, the object of the search is a proper factor. See Mr. Justice Jackson concurring in McDonald v. United States. Where the object of a search is a human being and from investigation it appears that

-13-

that human may well be on certain premises and be already injured only a fool would repair to a magistrate and debate probable cause -- where the stakes is a weapon or contraband or narcotics, yes, where it is a human life, no.

To demonstrate the absurdity of the logical extension of the defendant's position, let us hypothecate one factor to the circumstances as they existed -- Suppose that Mr. Gein had told the officers that he had shot Mrs. Worden and she was at his farm. If the defendant's analysis is correct the officers would be obliged to return to Wautoma, alert a magistrate, conduct a warrant hearing and obtain a warrant before entering Mr. Gein's farm.

It may be true as the poet has said that "the law is an ass" but not that much of one.

In the final analysis the Fourth Amendment means exactly what it says:

> "The right of the people to be secure in their persons, houses, papers, and effects, against un-reasonable searches and seizures, shall not be violated..."

The pivotal word is reasonable. The State submits that in the instant case the search was reasonable under the constitution of the United States and of Wisconsin, and the fruits thereof are therefore admissible.

Respectfully submitted,

ROBERT E. SUTTON
Special Assistant Attorney General

-13-

STATE OF WISCONSIN   )

)   SS:

COUNTY OF WAUSHARA   )

    IN THE CIRCUIT COURT OF WAUSHARA COUNTY

STATE OF WISCONSIN,   )

           Plaintiff,   )

)   No.

    vs.   )

EDWARD GEIN,   )

          Defendant.   )

    REPORT OF PROCEEDINGS at the hearing

of the above-entitled cause before the Honorable

ROBERT H. GOLLMAR, Judge of said Court, on the

7th day of November, A. D. 1968, at 9:00 o'clock

a.m.

        APPEARANCES:

           MR. HOWARD DUTCHER,
           District Attorney,
             appeared on behalf of the State;

           MR. ROBERT SUTTON,
           Assistant Attorney General,
             appeared on behalf of the State;

           MR. WILLIAM N. BELTER, and
           MR. DOMINIC FRINZI, Special Defense Counsel,
             appeared on behalf of the Defendant.

I N D E X

I N D E X

3

I N D E X

4

5

THE COURT: State versus Ed Gein. I assume,
Jerry, you have the appearances?

COURT REPORTER: Yes, sir.

THE COURT: Will the District Attorney read
the informations, please?

MR. DUTCHER: "State of Wisconsin, County of
Waushara. I, HOWARD DUTCHER, District Attorney
for Waushara County, Wisconsin, hereby inform the
Court that on the 16th day of November, 1957, at the
said County of Waushara, Wisconsin, Edward Gein
did with intent to steal by using force against the
person of Bernice Worden with intent to overcome
her physical power of resistance to the taking
and carrying away of the property of the said
Bernice Worden, feloniously rob and take from the
said Bernice Worden, the property of said Bernice
Worden, contrary to Section 943.32 of the Wisconsin
Statutes and against the peace and dignity of the
State of Wisconsin.

"Dated this 7th day of November, 1968, at
Wautoma, Wisconsin." Signed: Howard E. Dutcher,
District Attorney of Waushara County.

Count two: "State of Wisconsin, County of
Waushara. I, HOWARD DUTCHER, District Attorney
for Waushara County, Wisconsin, hereby inform the

6

107

Court that on the 16th day of November, 1957, at the
said County of Waushara, Wisconsin, Edward Gein did
feloniously cause the death of one Bernice Worden,
a human being, with intent to kill the said Bernice
Worden, contrary to Section 940.01 of the Wisconsin
Statutes, and against the peace and dignity of the
State of Wisconsin.

"Dated this 7th day of November, 1968,
at Wautoma, Wisconsin."

Signed: Howard Dutcher, District Attorney,
Waushara County, Wisconsin.

THE COURT: The informations are filed.

To this information do we have a plea?

MR. FRINZI: Your Honor, at this time, the
defendant, Edward Gein, would like to enter a plea
of not guilty, or not guilty by reason of insanity,
with reference to the robbery charge and also with
reference to the murder count.

And for the purposes of the record, I'd
like to ask the defendant, Mr. Gein -- you want to
stand up?

You understand the two charges that were
read by the District Attorney?

MR. GEIN: Right.

MR. FRINZI: One for robbery and one for

7

108

murder.

MR. GEIN: Yes. Right.

MR. FRINZI: Is it your intention that you want to enter a plea of not guilty, and not guilty by reason of insanity to both charges?

MR. GEIN: Yes.

MR. FRINZI: And that is your wish and desire?

MR. GEIN: Right.

MR. FRINZI: I am satisfied, your Honor, that the defendant is entering this plea with full knowledge here.

THE COURT: Very well. The pleas are accepted as to both counts.

MR. FRINZI: Now, if the Court please, before we proceed, in order to protect the record, we'd like to enter a waiver of trial by jury. That's been signed by the defendant, Edward Gein, and I would also like to tender the waiver to the State and ask that the State sign this waiver, because I believe the State does have a right to a jury trial if they so desire, or they have the same right to waive as the defendant has.

So, at this time I have two waivers prepared for each charge. If you will both sign them, and then I will have copies for you.

At this time, we'd like to file,   8

your Honor, the waiver signed by Edward Gein, and also by the State of Wisconsin, represented by Robert Sutton and Howard Dutcher.

THE COURT: Mr. Gein, you understand that under the Constitution of the United States of America, under the Constitution of the State of Wisconsin, you are entitled to have a jury --

MR. GEIN: Right.

THE COURT: -- of twelve people?

MR. GEIN: Right.

THE COURT: Of your peers to hear this case. You understand that that is your right under the law?

MR. GEIN: Right.

THE COURT: Knowing that that is your right, will you tell the Court whether or not you want this case tried by a jury, without a jury, or do you want a jury?

MR. GEIN: I believe I will have it tried before the Judge.

THE COURT: You are willing to give up that right to trial by jury that you have?

MR. GEIN: Right.

THE COURT: You understand that?

MR. GEIN: Right. Also on advice of Counsel.

9

MR. FRINZI: You discussed this with myself
and Mr. Belter at times?

MR. GEIN: Yes.

MR. FRINZI: And you have come to the conclusion
that you would like to have this tried by the Judge?

MR. GEIN: Right.

MR. FRINZI: Mr. Dutcher and I have exercised
no undue influence on you in order for you to say
that you want a trial by the Court rather then by
a jury?

MR. GEIN: Right.

MR. FRINZI: You understand that?

MR. GEIN: Right.

THE COURT: Very well, it is understood the
jury is waived, and the trial will be to the Court.

I was just going to ask the question:
Does the Court also understand that you are asking
for a bifurcated trial and you want to proceed
under the Schoffner Rule rather then the Esser
Rule?

MR. FRINZI: Yes.

We also have the proper papers that the
case calls for to perfect the record with the
waiver, and the election, as the Supreme Court calls
for in the Schoffner Case.

                                                    10

111

I'd like to give copies to both
Prosecutors here, one for each of you. If you
will sign the Admission of Service we will file
these with the Court.

Your Honor, we prepared separate waivers
and elections in each case -- in the robbery case
and in the murder case.

THE COURT: The State, I gather, has no
objection?

MR. SUTTON: No, your Honor.

I do note there is a request for
instructions, which I gather is superfluous since
there is no jury.

MR. FRINZI: At the time we were preparing,
we hadn't decided whether a jury trial was going
to come about, but if we don't proceed with the jury,
it becomes mute.

MR. SUTTON: All right.

MR. FRINZI: In the event we had a jury trial,
your Honor, this requirement had to be. I'd like
to file the first one in reference to the murder
charge.

Now, I'd like to tender the Admission of
Service on the robbery count.

Now, I'd like to file the Admission of

11

Service along with the waiver and election in the robbery count.

THE COURT: Are you ready?

MR. FRINZI: Your Honor, I'd also like to make a motion at this time, first of all, for a sequestration of witnesses. In other words, as the witnesses testify and are finished, they can remain in Court, but until such time, the witnesses be sequestrated.

Also, I'd like to make a motion for the method of proof in the case, since were operating under a bifurcated trial, that we will first proceed with the robbery and murder counts, and the Court will make its determination at the conclusion of that case, and then proceed after the finding in the murder and robbery counts on the issue of insanity, if we get that far.

THE COURT: Yes.

MR. SUTTON: We have no objection to that your Honor.

I would make one motion to consolidate the matters for trial, assuring the Court that the evidence relates to both charges.

THE COURT: Yes. I assume, Mr. Frinzi, that will be understood, that we will consolidate the

12

113

two counts for trial and proceed.

The Court further understands that we will take the testimony as to the question of guilty or not guilty first, and then if the Court finds the defendant guilty, we will then proceed into the insanity phase. At that time, under the Schoffner Rule, the Defense will assume the burden of proof and it will be up to them to go forward in the case.

MR. SUTTON: All right, your Honor.

MR. FRINZI: One more thing, your Honor: In that regard, on the second part, in the event we get to that point, since we have the burden of proof, we have elected to proceed under the American Law Institute Rule rather than the M'Naughten Rule.

THE COURT: Yes, it is so understood.

Any question about sequestering the witnesses?

MR. SUTTON: Yes, your Honor, I'd like Captain Schoephoester here.

Where we going to sequester them?

THE COURT: That's a good question. Mr. Chase, can we put them into the County Board room or Law Library?

MR. SUTTON: Mr. Murty may remain here, but

13

114

Captain Schoephoester may go with the Deputy.
And I'd like to advise the Sheriff that some of
my witnesses have not appeared yet in the Courthouse,
and they may try to come into the Court room, not
knowing about the order. So, if the Deputy will
keep his eyes open -- if anybody comes in, Officer,
will you ask them to leave.

SHERIFF BATTERMAN: Mr. Chase is going to be
a witness.

MR. SUTTON: I would move that he be an
exception to that rule since he is a bailiff.

THE COURT: You want him sequestered?

MR. FRINZI: Who is that?

THE COURT: Mr. Chase, my bailiff.

MR. FRINZI: No.

THE COURT: All right. It's understood Mr.
Chase may remain here.

MR. FRINZI: We put him in the category, like
in other trials, that he's one of the aiding
officers that usually is permitted to sit at the
Counsel table.

THE COURT: We'll follow the Milwaukee court
rule - there is also a detective at the right hand
of the Prosecutor. At least that is my experience.

Now, you want to make an opening statement?

14

MR. SUTTON: No, your Honor, State waives the opening statement.

MR. FRINZI: We will reserve our right to any opening statement until the prosecution presents its case, your Honor.

THE COURT: Very well. I permitted that in Brown County, and I apparently violated the local ground rule, and the other Judges were a little shook about that, but I did it anyway.

All right, Mr. Sutton, you want to call your first witness?

MR. SUTTON: Mr. Leon Murty, please.

LEON MURTY,

called as a witness herein, having been first duly sworn, was examined and testified as follows:

DIRECT EXAMINATION

BY

MR. SUTTON:

Q What is your name, Sir?

A Leon Murty.

Q Where do you live?

A Wild Rose, Wisconsin.

Q And what is your occupation or employment?

A Auto body repair.

Q Now, I direct your attention to November of

15

116

1957, how were you employed at that time?

A Village Marshall for the Village of Wild Rose, and also Deputy Sheriff for Waushara County.

Q And who was the Sheriff at that time, if you know?

A Arthur Schley.

Q Now, I direct your attention to November 16, 1957, were you so employed as a Deputy Sheriff on that day?

A Yes.

Q Were you on duty that day?

A In the afternoon, later in the afternoon, yes.

Q Did you have occasion to go to the Village of Plainfield to the Worden Hardware Store on that day?

A Yes, I did.

Q Would you describe the circumstances that brought you to the Worden Store?

A Well, I got a call from the Sheriffs Department that the Sheriff and Arnold Fritz was at Plainfield at the Worden's Hardware and they wanted me up there as soon as I could get there.

Q How did you proceed to the Worden Hardware Store?

16

117

A   I drove up there.

Q   Did anyone go with you?

A   No.

Q   Approximately what time on November 16, 1957, did you arrive at the Worden Hardware Store?

A   Well, that would be supper time, or just -- probably just about dark.

Q   When you arrived at the store, who if anyone was there?

A   Arthur Schley and Deputy Fritz.

MR. FRINZI: I can't hear you.

THE WITNESS: A   Arthur Schley and Deputy Fritz.

MR. FRINZI: Fritz?

THE WITNESS: Yes.

MR. SUTTON: And --

THE WITNESS: A -- and Frank Worden.

Q   And, had you known Frank Worden prior to that day?

A   Yes, I had.

Q   And when you arrived at the premises did you go into the store?

A   I started to go in, and Frank Worden met me at the door.

Q   And what if anything did Frank Worden say

17

to you?

MR. FRINZI: Object to that as hearsay.

THE COURT: Sustained.

MR. SUTTON: Your Honor, at this juncture I would like to make an offer of proof and an argument in regard to this particular statement of Frank Worden's and other evidence which I hope to elicit from this witness as to statements made by Frank Worden on that afternoon of November 16, 1957. I propose to demonstrate to the Court that this testimony is admissible under the res gestae theory as adopted by the Wisconsin Supreme Court in Rudzinski versus Warner, 16 Wis. (2d) 241, and accepted in a criminal case in 1967 in State versus Smith at 36 Wis. (2d) 584, and as further amplified in Cossette versus Lepp, 38 Wis. (2d) 392.

It is my understanding from the Smith Case and from the Rudzinski Case that the Wisconsin Supreme Court has accepted Rule 512 A.L.I. Model Code of Evidence which indicates that -- and I quote now from the rule which is cited in both the Smith Case and the Rudzinski Case:

"Evidence of a hearsay statement is admissible if the judge

18

finds that the hearsay statement was
made (a) while the declarant" -- the
person giving the statement --"was
perceiving the event or condition
which the statement narrates or
describes or explains, or immediately
thereafter, or (b) while the declarant
was under the stress of a nervous
excitement caused by his perception
of the event or condition which the
statements narrates or describes or
explains."

There is further discussion in the
Smith Case and Rudzinski with regard to the
wide discretion and latitude given a judge to
determine the irrelevance of the testimony and
whether the rule should be applied, and I submit
that under both (a) and (b) of Rule 512 of the
A.L.I. I can demonstrate to this Court that
this testimony is admissible. It becomes somewhat self explaining.

I would ask the Court to allow me to
elicit the testimony and reserve a ruling on it.
And I make an offer of proof that it is the
discovery of the fact that his mother was missing,

19

120

and the circumstances and physical circumstances
in his store that he made these statements, and
secondly, that Mr. Worden, at the time he made
these statements, was under the stress of nervous
excitement caused by the perceiving of all these
circumstances, and that by the examination of all
of the circumstances, I submit that the Court will
find that the statements made by Mr. Worden at
that time have great probative value, and are not
suspect as most hearsay declarations are as to
their veracity.

And I submit that the way I can best
demonstrate this to the Court is to the allow
the witness to relate what Mr. Worden told him
that evening and apply the rule whether under
all these circumstances it is applicable.

THE COURT: Any comment, Mr. Frinzi?

MR. FRINZI: Your Honor, we object to the
argument that Counsel for the State has made here
for the simple reason that no proper foundation
has been laid here to fall within the scope and
purviewoof the exception to the hearsay rule as
Mr. Sutton has stated.

All we have here at this point is this
witness, Mr. Murty, meeting Mr. Worden at the

20

door of this hardware store. That's all. There has to be more than that under the Res Gestae Rule, and he'd have to lay the foundation before the Court can even permit him to make an offer of proof.

THE COURT: Well, I think that's right, Mr. Sutton. I think you have to lay some foundation to establish you come within the exception.

MR. SUTTON: But the fact of the matter is with this particular testimony the foundation is linked within the statements themselves. I can have Mr. Murty describe the premises first, but from the standpoint of chronolgy, it suffers a little, but I can lay foundation.

THE COURT: The Court will withdraw it's ruling and hold the ruling open. I will permit you to examine the witness subject to the objection with the understanding it will be stricken if the Court determines it doesn't come within the exception.

MR. SUTTON: At the conclusion of the testimony I presume the Court would like to probably -- I'm sure the Court concedes perhaps that I'm accurately citing the law --

THE COURT: I trust you are.

21

MR. SUTTON: -- would like to review these cases before he makes a final ruling.

MR. FRINZI: I'd like the Court also to further reserve his ruling subject to cross examination by the Defense.

THE COURT: It will be so understood, and the Court will also like to glance at those cases before I make a final ruling.

Proceed.

MR. SUTTON: You may answer the question.

What did Mr. Worden say to you when you met him at the door?

MR. FRINZI: Your Honor, excuse me. I am going to make my objection to each question rather than an overall objection.

THE COURT: YOu don't have to unless you desire to for the record. The Court is perfectly willing to have it understood that you object to this entire line of questioning.

MR. FRINZI: All right, then it will be a continuing objection to all of this hearsay testimony.

THE COURT: That's right.

MR. SUTTON: All right.

THE WITNESS: A Frank Worden said -- I

22

forget just what I said to him, if he got a buck
or something -- I didn't know what happened --
and he says, "Never mind the deer hunting,
something happened here - I'm afraid something
happened to Mama. Come in and look".

MR. SUTTON: Q And then did you enter the
store?

A Yes.

Q Would you describe what you observed in
the interior of the store, if anything?

A Well there was some -- something on the
floor that looked to me like it could be blood and
also like something had been dragged thru it out
to the back room.

Q Now, at this juncture did you have a
further conversation with Mr. Worden?

A No. I think I talked to the Sheriff
then.

Q Now, while you were in the store, did
Mr. Worden appear to you to be excited or nervous?

MR. FRINZI: Object to that as leading and
suggestive.

MR. SUTTON: That's part of the foundation.

THE COURT: You're leading but he may answer.

THE WITNESS: A Yes, he was.

23

124

MR. SUTTON: Q How did he appear?

THE WITNESS: A Worried and excited.

MR. FRINZI: I move that the word "worried" be stricken as a conclusion.

THE COURT: I think it is, but it may stand.

MR. SUTTON: Q Did Mr. Worden make any further statements to you with regard to your investigation at that time?

MR. FRINZI: I'm going to move that the word "investigation" be stricken. There is nothing in the record or evidence to indicate any investigation, your Honor. It's assuming a fact not in evidence.

THE COURT: Whatever he was doing there. He may answer.

THE WITNESS: A I talked to Mr. Worden, yes, if he had any suspicions of anybody - if anything happened to his mother.

MR. SUTTON: Q What did Mr. Worden say to you?

A He said, "yes" that he did have.

Q Did he say anything further on that subject?

A That there was a certain party who had been in the store different times bothering his mother, and asking her to go roller skating with

24

him, or to movies, and that this party had been
in the store the day before and asked him if he
was going deer hunting the next day, and Frank
told him, "yes," and also that he was going to
buy some anti-freeze or alcohol for his car.

Q By "he," you mean the party that Mr.
Worden was telling you about?

A Yes.

Q Who was that person?

A I finally got to ask him who it was, and
he said Eddie Gein.

Q And did you have any further -- strike that.
Did you make any further investigation on the
premises with regard to this sale of anti-freeze?

A Yes.

Q Would you describe that?

A I asked him if they kept a record of any
sales slips or anything, and he said, yes, they did,
and there was two sales made, one of anti-freeze, and
one of -- some kind of pipe - some fitting or something

Q And how did you and Mr. Worden determine
that there had been a sale of anti-freeze made?

A By checking the slips.

Q Where were the slips in the store?

A Well, the counter where the cash register

25

usually set, next to it.

Q Was there a cash register on the premises?

A No.

Q Did you have any discussion with Mr.
Worden regarding the cash register?

A He said the cash register had been taken -
gone.

Q He advised you that the cash register was
missing from the premises also?

A Yes.

Q What if anything did he advise you with
regard to whether his mother had been present the
day before when Mr. Gein made the statements about
hunting and about the anti-freeze?

A No. He didn't.

MR. FRINZI: What was that answer?

THE COURT: He said "no, he didn't".

MR. SUTTON: Q Did Mr. Worden tell you where
he had been that day?

A Well, only that I asked him if he got a
buck when I first talked to him or had any luck.

Q Did you ask him that question?

A Well, I knew he was a deer hunter, and I
figured he was out.

Q Was Mrs. Bernice Worden on those premises

26

127

at that time?

A No, not that I saw.

Q Was there any other conversation that you had with Mr. Worden at that time in the store?

A Well in the back room, when we went out in the back room, the pick-up truck was gone - the service truck that they use. It drives right in the back of the store to the garage - the work shop. That's all that I can remember.

MR. FRINZI: I move the answer be stricken as not responsive to the question. The question was: Was there any other conversation, not anything about a truck.

MR. SUTTON: I believe that objection is reserved to the party asking the question, your Honor.

THE COURT: I think so too.

MR. SUTTON: Now, at this juncture I will go into another area that is not related to the Res Gestae statements at the store, so if Mr. Frinzi at this time would like to cross examine on that particular issue --

THE COURT: Go ahead, Mr. Frinzi, if you want to.

MR. FRINZI: I'll reserve my right to cross

27

examination until this witness is completely finished.

THE COURT: Very well.

MR. SUTTON: Q Mr. Murty, did you have occasion at any time on November 16 or 17th, 1957, to go to Mr. Gein's home?

THE WITNESS: A Yes, I did.

Q And about what time did you go to the home?

A Well, the first time -- I'd have to make a guess -- I'd say 7:00 -- 6:30 - 7:00 o'clock.

Q Did you have occasion to go there later than that?

A Yes.

Q About what time was that?

A Early the next morning.

Q By "early," do you mean by dawn?

MR. FRINZI: Object to leading this witness your Honor.

THE COURT: It's somewhat leading, but he may answer.

THE WITNESS: A Wait a minute. That isn't right. I went back there, I'd say, an hour and a half - two hours afterwards. That would be 9:30 - 10:00 o'clock - somewheres in there.

28

129

Q   Did you have occasion, while on those premises to search any area for the cash register?

A   The next afternoon, yes.

Q   That was on the 17th?

A   Yes.

Q   What time was that ?

A   Well --

Q   Approximately.

A   It would have to be a guess. I'd have to say 2:00 o'clock.

Q   Would you state whether or not you discovered a cash register on Mr. Gein's premises?

A   Yes, I did.

MR. SUTTON: Mark these, please?

(Whereupon, said documents wer
marked Plaintiff's Exhibits
Nos. 1, 2 & 3 for Identification.)

Mr. Murty, I show you what has been marked State's Exhibit 1 for identification. What is that?

A   Photograph.

Q   What is that a photograph of?

A   Of a farm home, I would say.

Q   Do you recognize that farm home?

29

130

A   It looks like Edward Gein's house. Yes.

Q   Does it appear to be the farm home as it
appeared in November of 1957?

MR. FRINZI: Object to leading and suggestive,
your Honor.

THE COURT: He may answer.

THE WITNESS: A Yes.

MR. SUTTON: Q I show you what has been
marked Exhibit 2 for Identification. What is
that?

THE WITNESS: A The same house.

Q   Also a photograph?

A   Yes.

Q   I show you what has been marked Exhibit 3
for Identification and ask you what that is?

A   Another photograph of the same house.

Q   Now, Mr. Murty, would you tell me whether or
not the cash register you testified was recovered
from the premises is depicted in State's Exhibits 1,
2, and 3?

A   Yes.

MR. SUTTON: Your witness.

                CROSS EXAMINATION

                BY

                MR. FRINZI:

                                            30

Q   Now, Mr. Murty, what time would you say that you received this call to go to the Worden Hardware Store?

A   Well, I would say close to 5:00 o'clock one way or the other, maybe. Around there.

Q   Your not sure?

A   I couldn't be absolutely sure.

Q   Do you know what time you arrived at the Hardware Store - the Worden Hardware Store?

A   Just after it got dark I know.

Q   Do you know about what time it was?

A   That would be another guess. 5:30, I'd say.

Q   Where were you at the time you got the call to go to the Worden Hardware Store?

A   I had just arrived at my home. Just got there.

Q   Where was your home in 1957?

A   Wild Rose.

Q   How far was that from the Worden Hardware Store?

A   About fourteen miles.

Q   After you got the call, did you immediately proceed to go to the Worden Hardware Store.

A   Yes.

31

Q   About how much time did it take you to get there?

A   Oh, 20 minutes - 25 maybe.

Q   I see. And, when you got there who if anyone did you see at the Hardware Store outside of the store?

A   I don't recall seeing anyone outside, I don't believe.

Q   Were you the first one at the Hardware Store, or was someone else there?

A   No. The Sheriff -- Sheriff Schley and Deputy Fritz were the first ones called there, if that's what you mean.

Q   My question is: Was anyone there before you got there? Was Schley and Fritz at the Hardware Store when you arrived?

A   Yes.

Q   Where were they?

A   Inside.

Q   They were inside?

A   Yes.

Q   And you were outside?

A   Yes.

Q   Where was Frank Worden when you arrived?

A   He met me at the door.

32

133

Q He wasn't inside the store? He was at the door outside?

A He was inside the store, and when I come up to the door he opened the door, and that's where I first saw him.

Q That's where you first saw him, at the door?

A Yes.

Q Did you go inside the store when you first saw him or did you stay outside with him?

A No, I went in.

Q And you had conversations with Mr. Worden inside the store - Frank Worden - inside the store?

A Yes.

Q And at the time you had these conversations that you testified to, was anyone else present besides you and Mr. Worden?

A The Sheriff and Deputy Arnold Fritz.

Q Pardon?

A The Sheriff, Schley, and Deputy Arnold Fritz.

Q Now, who did the talking? Who asked Frank Worden any questions? Did you ask him, or the Sheriff ask him?

A At that time I asked him.

Q I see. And the Sheriff was present?

33

A   Yes.

Q   And Deputy Fritz was present?

A   Yes.

Q   Do you know if anybody took out any notebooks; and took down the conversation that occurred?

A   Not that I recall.

Q   To your knowledge there were no notes made of your conversation with Frank Worden?

A   No, not that I know of.

Q   In other words, your testifying as to what you remember? You havent looked back at any reports?

A   No.

Q   And to your knowledge no reports were made?

A   No.

Q   And you didn't know what the conditions were before you got there at that store, did you - whether the door was open or closed?

A   No.

Q   You just found Fritz -- Deputy Fritz and Sheriff Schley, and Frank Worden inside the store?

A   Yes.

Q   Now, do you know if anyone had been to that store prior to Frank Worden, Deputy Schley --

34

Scheriff Schley, or Deputy Fritz?

A   No, I don't know.

Q   How long were you at the store?

A   Well, that would be another guess.   I
didn't check any time or anything.

Q   Well, approximately. Was it ten minutes -
five minutes?

A   Oh, yes, longer then that. Half-hour or hour
maybe.

Q   Now, over how long a period of time did
you talk to Frank Worden?

A   Well, I didn't talk to him all the time,
but I probably asked him a question now and then
while looking things over.

Q   Well, did you talk over a period of an
hour?

A   No.

Q   About half-hour?

A   Put together it wouldn't be even ten
minutes.

Q   But on and off you talked to him?

A   Yes.

Q   How long a period was this that you talked
to him on and off?

                                            35

136

A I'd say about an half-hour, but I didn't
talk to him all that time. If I asked him all
the questions right in a row it would be about
ten minutes maybe.

Q On and off you talked to him around a
period of a hour?

A That would be a guess. I don't know.

Q Did you know Frank Worden before this day?

A Yes.

Q And did Mr. Worden talk to you in his usual
tone of voice?

A No.

Q Well, what was different?

A Well, he was pretty worried about something
could have happened to his mother.

Q But that was an expression. But how did
that affect his voice? Was his voice the same as
it usually was?

A He talked fast and louder.

Q What else did you observe about the tone
of his voice?

A I don't think anything.

Q Pardon?

A I don't think anything.

Q Now, did Mr. Worden deliberate in his

36

conversation with you?

MR. SUTTON: Object. That calls for a characterisation.

THE COURT: What?

MR. FRINZI: Deliberate. Was he slow sometimes in his talk to you?

THE COURT: He's asking you if he was slow.

THE WITNESS: A No, I wouldn't say so.

MR. FRINZI: Q Pardon?

A I wouldn't say he was slow.

Q Did he appear to be thinking when he was answering your questions?

A Sure.

MR. SUTTON: Object, that's indefinite and calls for a conclusion.

MR. FRINZI: He said he looked worried.

THE COURT: But we didn't let that in.

MR. FRINZI: If I put my head down like Judges do, that's a sign their thinking.

THE COURT: Sometimes it's a sign their sleeping, but go ahead.

MR. FRINZI: Q Now, Mr. Murty, you say you were Deputy Sheriff, right?

A Yes.

Q And you arrested people, have you not in

37

138

the past while you were acting as a Deputy Sheriff?

A Yes.

Q And you have seen people under arrest who were excited, didn't you?

A Yes.

Q Do they always tell the truth?

MR. SUTTON: Object. That's immaterial.

THE COURT: Sustained. Don't answer.

MR. FRINZI: Q Now, did Frank Worden help you, and Sheriff Schley, and Deputy Fritz in the investigation that you people were making in the store?

A Well, he was walking around there looking around all the time, yes, to see if anything was missing.

Q How old was Mr. Worden at that time?

A I wouldn't know. Thirty, maybe.

Q He was a Deputy Sheriff, wasn't he, Mr. Frank Worden? He was a Deputy Sheriff like you were, wasn't he, in 1957?

A I think he could have been, yes.

Q Now, did you say that Mr. Worden looked around the store to see if there was anything missing?

A Yes.

38

139

Q   Did he go anywhere in the store to make
an inventory to look and see what items may or
may not have been missing?

A   Well, I know he was the one that noticed
the cash register was gone.

Q   He was looking around the store to see if
anything was missing?

A   Yes.

Q   Did he tell you that?

A   I figured that's what he was looking for.

Q   Was he running around or did he walk?

A   He kept right on walking right along.

Q   He was looking around to see if there was anything missing?

A   Yes.

Q   Now, you said that he told you that Mr.
Gein was supposed to have been bothering his mother?

A   Yes.

Q   Now, you were Deputy Sheriff, right?

A   Yes.

Q   Were any of these complaints ever made to
the Sheriff's office or local police department
here?

A   Not that I know of.

Q   Any record of any complaints concerning

39

140

Mr. Gein bothering Mrs. Worden?

A Not that I know of.

Q You don't know of any?

A No.

Q You said there were two sales slips
in the store?

A Yes.

Q Did you see them?

A Yes, I did.

Q Did they have any names on these sales
slips as to who made the purchase?

A No.

Q In other words, that was blank?

A Yes.

Q From those sales slips, you don't know,
or anyone knows, to whom this merchandise was
sold, isn't that correct?

A No, sir.

Q Now, what made you say that it appears that
something had been dragged over something that you
said looked like blood?

A Well, there was -- you could see plain on
the floor something -- two drag marks or scuff
marks.

40

141

Q   Do you know where in the store these
marks that your talking about began?

A   Yes. I couldn't say the exact spot, but
it was just inside the back door a little ways
where you go out the back room.

Q   How large would you say that store was?

A   It's a pretty good size building.

Q   The store itself?

A   Oh, 40 by 50 maybe. Just a guess.

Q   Is it one large room - the store?

A   Yes, the front part, yes.

Q   Was there a counter in there?

A   Yes. A number of counters.

Q   How long would you estimate the counter
to be?

THE COURT: Number of counters, he said.

MR. SUTTON: Q How many were there?

THE WITNESS: A Showcases or counters
with stuff piled on them.

Q   How many were there?

A   I wouldn't know.

Q   Were there two, three?

A   I'd say at least two, maybe three showcases
or counters, whatever you call them. Stuff for sale

41

was piled up on them.

Q Where does that back door that you testified
to lead to.

A To the back part of the store where they
kept parts and did repair work. Kind of a work
shop, I'd say.

Q Now did you have occasion to observe a
rack that had a gun display on it in the store?

A Yes.

Q And where was that rack with relation to
the back door you just testified to? How far was
that gun rack to the back door?

A Well I don't know just exactly how far,
but the gun rack was against the rear wall of the
store, and I think if you were standing facing the
door it was to the right.

Q How far would you estimate the distance
from where you are now? How far would you estimate
in distance from where you are in relation to this
room?

THE COURT: To what?

MR. FRINZI: From where the gun rack was to
the door - to that back door.

THE WITNESS: A Oh, I'd say from here to the

42

corner of Mrs. McComb's desk. About that far.

MR. FRINZI: Judge, you want to estimate the distance so we have something in the record?

THE COURT: You guess.

THE WITNESS: It would be about eight - nine feet, something like that. Can't be sure of that either. I didn't do any measuring.

MR. FRINZI: Q How far would you say that this gun display rack was from where this area that you said looked like or appeared like blood? How far was that distance?

A Ten - twelve feet, something like that.

Q First of all, let me ask you this: Did you investigate the store?

A Oh, I looked around, sure.

Q You looked around the store? What if anything did you see other then what you testified to on direct examination about something that looked like, or appeared like, blood?

A Do you mean if I saw any more of it, or --

Q Did you see anything else besides what looked like blood?

A No.

Q That is all you saw is what looked like blood?

43

A   Yes.

Q   Did you see any bullet holes in the wall?

A   No.

Q   Did you see any guns off the rack?

A   I saw one gun that was changed around in the rack.

Q   First of all, did you know where the gun display or rack was before you walked into the store?

A   Yes, I think I did.

Q   How did you know?

A   Before Schley was in I was Sheriff and I was there at a burglary.

Q   I'm talking on the day of November 16.

A   Oh, no.

Q   1957.

A   No.

Q   You don't know what the condition of that gun rack was?

A   When you asked me before, you didn't say when.

MR. SUTTON: It's argumenative.   He does know what the condition was when he observed it.

THE COURT: His original answer may stand.   You didn't limit it as to when.   44

MR. FRINZI: Let's get the record clear. He testified, your Honor, that he saw a gun that was on the -- let's skip this testimony:

Now what did you see, or observe about the gun rack?

THE WITNESS: A Well, there was this one gun that was placed in the gun rack different than the rest of them. There was a number of guns in the gun rack.

Q That's what you observed?

A Yes.

Q You don't know how it got there?

A No.

Q You didn't know whether it was that way earlier in the day?

A No.

Q You didn't know whether that gun was in that condition the day before?

A No.

Q Did you handle that gun?

A No.

Q Did anyone in your presence -- did you see anyone in your presence handle that gun?

A No.

45

Q   Was that gun ever taken off the rack while
you were there to your knowledge?

A   Not at that time.

Q   Pardon? Did you see anyone touch that gun?

A   Not at that time.

Q   Well, did you see anyone touch it at any other
time?

A   Later on the men from the Crime Lab.

Q   When was that?

A   Now, I couldn't be sure about the time.

Q   Was it on the same night?

A   No, it would be the next day.

Q   I see. It was the next day?

A   Yes.

Q   When on the next day?

A   That I couldn't say - the time.

Q   Now, were you present when that gun
was taken off the rack the next day?

A   Yes.

Q   Did you see anyone take that gun out of
there?

A   Out of the rack?

Q   Yes.

A   Yes.

Q   Who did you see take that gun out of there?

46

A I'm quite sure it was Alan Wilimovsky.

Q You saw him take it out?

A Yes.

Q How did he take that gun out?

A Well, a handkerchief and a pencil.

Q Now, was there any lock on the gun rack or was it just out in the open -- the guns?

A In the open.

Q In the open?

A Yes.

Q I see. Now, you say you have been in that store before and you saw this gun display?

A Yes.

Q You saw customers take the guns off the wall and handle them and look at them before making a purchase?

MR. SUTTON: Object.

THE COURT: He may answer.

THE WITNESS: A I don't know. I saw it in other places, but I don't know if I saw it in that place.

Q The guns were in the open? It wasn't in a glass case? You could look at that gun if you were going to make a purchase, right?

A Yes.

47

Q Now, did you know Ed Gein prior to November 17, 1957?

A I had saw him once.

Q And, do you know whether or not Ed Gein owned a gun?

A No, I didn't.

Q Now, to get back to this gun display here, you said that you were at the Worden Hardware Store on the night of November 17, 1957, for about a hour - hour and a half, right?

MR. SUTTON: Your Honor --

MR. FRINZI: I'll withdraw the question.

How long were you there?

THE WITNESS: A I don't know.

Q How long were you at the Worden Hardware Store from the time you first arrived?

A I'd say half hour to a hour.

Q And then did you leave?

A Yes.

Q Who did you leave at the store?

A Sheriff Schley, Deputy Fritz, and Frank Worden were there.

Q Now did you have occasion to come back to the store anymore that night on November 17, 1957?

MR. SUTTON: Now, I object to that because

149

he's got the wrong date.

MR. FRINZI: November 16.

THE WITNESS: That's what it should have been on the other question too.

MR. FRINZI: Q Now, you went there on the 16th?

A Yes.

Q You went there on the 16th the first time?

A Yes.

Q You were there a half hour?

A Something like that.

Q And then you left?

A I did.

Q Did you come back anymore the night of the 16th?

A I came back there, stopped outside, but I didn't go in.

Q How long did you remain there?

A Outside?

Q Yes.

A Just stopped and took right off again.

Q I see. Did you see anybody in the Worden Store at the time you stopped by?

A I didn't even check to look.

Q You don't know if the place was padlocked

49

or barricaded?

A No.

Q Did you know whether or not there was a
guard or Deputy Sheriff outside that store guarding
it?

A I noticed a car there but I didn't see --

Q Who's car was it?

A Arnold Fritz.

Q You didn't notice whether he was inside ?

A No.

Q Did you have occasion to return that
evening anymore near the store or in the store?

A No.

Q Pardon?

A No.

Q Did you have occasion to come back to that
store on November 17th, the next day?

A Sometimes the next day I was there.

Q What time would you say? Was it in the
morning or in the afternoon?

A I'd say it would be in the afternoon.

Q So, what happened from the last time when
you past by the store on the night of November 16th
to the afternoon of the 17th, you don't know what
happened to that store?

50

A   No.

Q   Pardon?

A   No, I don't.

Q   You don't know whether that store was padlocked, do you?

A   No.

Q   You don't know whether it was guarded all
night, do you?

A   Not that I saw myself, no.

Q   You don't know whether the premises or the
area was barricaded off?

A   No.

Q   Pardon?

A   No.

Q   Were any signs posted that no one was to
enter this store?

A   No.

Q   Now, did this store, to your knowledge, sell
bullets?

A   Bullets?

Q   Yes.

A   Yes.

Q   Do you know to your knowledge where these
bullets were kept?

A   No. I saw them there, but I couldn't say

51

where.

Q You don't know where they were kept?

A No.

Q That night when you were in the store did anyone -- did Mr. Worden or anyone else show you where the bullets -- any bullets were?

A No.

Q Now, let me ask you this, Mr. Murty: Do you know where Frank Worden is today?

A No, I don't.

Q When was the last time you saw or heard from Frank Worden?

MR. SUTTON: Object. It's immaterial.

MR. FRINZI: It's very material. It's the State's Case. If they know where he is, they have an obligation to bring him here.

THE WITNESS: I haven't seen him in five or six years.

MR. FRINZI: Q You haven't seen or heard from him in five or six years?

A No.

Q Now, did you receive any information from anyone whether or not the bullets in the Worden Store had been tampered with?

A No.

52

153

Q You didn't hear that from anybody?

A No.

Q Mr. Worden never told you that, did he?

A No.

Q Pardon?

A No.

Q Now, getting back to your testimony earlier, Mr. Murty, you testified something about roller skating. I didn't quite understand you. What was that conversation you had with Mr. Worden?

A After we had looked things over, I asked him if he had any suspicions of anybody that might harm his mother, and he said, "yes, I do have one" -- I don't know if he said person or party -- "that I don't like. He's been hanging around here, and bothering my mother to go roller skating with her."

Q What is that?

A To go roller skating with her or go to dances or go to shows.

Q Did he say that they go roller skating?

A No, he said this party had been bothering his mother to go, wanting to go with her.

Q Did he say he heard this party say to his mother that he wanted to go roller skating?

A Yes.

53

Q From who did he hear that?

A He heard when this party asked his mother, the way I understood it.

Q Did he definitely say to you that he heard Edward Gein tell his mother, or ask his mother, to go roller skating with her?

A No, I don't think he said it that way.

Q Did he say he heard Ed Gein tell his mother that he wanted to take her to the show? Did he tell you that in those words?

A Not that way, no.

Q Did he tell you that he heard Edward Gein ask his mother to go dancing?

A He didn't even mention the name, he said "party."

Q Did he say he heard his mother talking to the party that he heard these words from?

A No.

Q He just said he had a suspicion?

A Yes.

Q And he didn't like the guy?

A He said this person -- I don't know whether he heard it.

Q But he said he didn't like Edward Gein?

A He didn't like him doing it.

54

Q   Did he say he didn't like him?

A   He didn't like him doing that.

Q   But, he didn't tell you he heard or seen Edward Gein ask his mother to go dancing, or go to the movies, or roller skating?

A   No.

Q   Now, do you know, or remember, whether or not there was a counter between the gun rack and what you said appeared like blood - the spot that you said looked like blood?

A   Well, partly between, maybe. There was a walk-way around where you could walk around the ends of them.

Q   Now, you don't know, Mr. Murty, whether or not, after you left the store, whether or not Deputy Fritz or Sheriff Schley touched that gun that you said was placed in the rack?

A   No.

Q   You don't know whether or not they touched it?

A   No.

Q   But you do know nobody did anything about checking any evidence of what was in the Worden Store?

A   You mean writing --

55

Q No, checking it, or setting it aside, or barricading the evidence there.

A No.

Q Now, were you present when the men from the State Crime Laboratory came here to Plainfield?

A They came to the Gein residence first.

Q But, were you present when they went to the Worden Store?

A I was there, but I don't know whether I was there when they first went in or not.

Q Did you see them take pictures of the Worden Store?

A Seems as though I did.

Q But no pictures were taken by the Sheriff's office that night of the Worden's store?

A Not that I know of.

Q Now, were any pictures taken by the Sheriff's office or Crime Laboratory of the State of Wisconsin inside the Worden store on the 16th or 17th day of November that you know of?

A Not that I know of.

Q Now, I believe you testified on direct examination that you had been out to the Worden Store sometime before November 16th and 17th of 1957, is that correct?

You had been out to the Worden Store before?

A Yes, a number of times.

Q And, I thought I understood you to say that you had been called there to investigate an alledged burglary at the Worden Store?

A Yes.

Q And, how long ago prior to the 16th and 17th day of November, 1957, was that?

MR. SUTTON: Object.

THE COURT: He may answer.

THE WITNESS: A I wouldn't know, but I'd say it was six months or something like that.

MR. FRINZI: Q Prior to November 57?

A I wouldn't know for sure.

Q At that time that you received that complaint on this burglary to investigate this burglary at the Worden Store was Mr. Gein ever charged with that burglary?

A No.

Q Was he ever suspected of that burglary?

A No.

Q Was he ever interrogated concerning that burglary?

A No.

MR. SUTTON: Object.

MR. DUTCHER: Object.

57

THE COURT: That may stand, but I think you covered it.

MR. FRINZI: Q First of all, Mr. Murty, did you have occasion to look at the back door that you testified to on both Direct and Cross Examination? Did you have occasion to look at that door?

THE WITNESS: A The back door of what?

Q Of the store where you said this back door was near what looked like some blood. There was a back door there you said.

A Yes.

Q Did you have occasion to look at that door?

A I think when I was there the door was open.

Q So, you don't know what the condition of that door was before you got there, whether it was open or closed?

A No.

Q Now, Mr. Murty, do you recall whether or not you went to the Gein home on the night of November 16, 1957?

A Yes, I did.

Q And when was the first time to your knowledge that you went there?

A You mean the time?

Q Pardon?

159

A   You mean the time?

Q   Yes, the first time you went to the Gein home the night of November 16, 1957.

A   I'd have to guess.   It would be shortly after supper, 7:00 o'clock,   somewhere around in there.

Q   Did you go inside the home?

A   The first time yes.

Q   Did you take anything from the home the first time you went in it?

A   No.

Q   Did you go back the second time?

A   Yes.

Q   And how long after did you go into the home the second time? Was it ten minutes, half-hour?

A   I'd guess it would be 10:00 o'clock, somewheres around there.

Q   Three hours later?

A   Couple hours later.

Q   Did you take anything out of the Gein home the second time you went there?

A   Yes.

Q   Is it a fact that you took a small calibre revolver from his home?

A   Yes.

Q   And you didn't have a search warrant when   59

you took that revolver out of the house?

A No, I did not.

Q Did you determine whether or not Ed Gein owned that gun?

A No, I didn't.

Q When you took this gun out of the Gein home, how did you take that gun?

A I picked it up with a handkerchief.

Q Had you touched it before?

A No.

Q Do you know whether anyone touched it before you got there?

A No, I don't know.

Q You put it in a handkerchief, and then what did you do with it?

A Gave it to the sheriff.

Q You don't know whether it was inventoried?

A No.

Q When you turned it over to the sheriff, was there a marking put on the gun?

A Not that I saw, no.

Q You don't know what the sheriff did with the gun?

A I understood that he turned it over to the

Crime Lab.

Q But you don't know that?

A No.

Q Whether he inventoried it you don't know?

A No.

Q But you know that when you turned it over to Sheriff Schley there was no marking made on that gun or identification, or there was no inventory made of that gun?

A Not that I saw.

Q Now, did you have occasion to look at that gun or examine it?

A Well, just enough to know it was a gun is all.

Q Did you have a chance to determine whether or not that gun was in working order?

A No.

Q You don't know whether that gun was in working order?

A No.

Q Where is Sheriff Schley today?

A He passed away awhile back.

Q You didn't have permission or consent from Ed Gein to take that small calibre gun out of his home, did you?

61

A   No, I didn't.

Q   Nor did you have permission or consent from
Ed Gein to go into the home on the night of November 16,
1957, at both times that you went there?

A   No, I didn't.

Q   The fact of the matter is Mr. Gein was not
on the premises?

A   No.

Q   Was he on the premises or wasn't he?

A   No, he wasn't.

Q   Now, where would you say the largest
accumulation of what looked like blood -- where
was that inside the store in relation to the back
door?

A   If he was standing in the back of the door
facing into the store part, it would be a little to
the right of the door. I don't know, 7 - 8 feet -
something like that.

Q   In relation to this gun rack or gun display,
how far from the gun rack was the largest accumulation
of what looked like blood? How many feet?

A   Eight - nine feet, I'd say.

Q   Would you estimate to the Court how large
or how big this gun rack was? How many feet would
you say this gun rack was?

62

163

A   Just about as long as that desk that you
got there, something like that.

Q   How many feet is that, Mr. Murty?

A   Five feet.

Q   Now, did the gun rack stand up against the
wall?

A   Yes.

MR. FRINZI: That's all for the time being, your
Honor, and I'd like to ask the Court to have this
witness available throughout the trial.

MR. SUTTON: I have few questions on re-direct.

RE-DIRECT EXAMINATION

BY

MR. SUTTON:

Q   Mr. Murty, do you know where Mr. Gein was
on November 17, 1957?

A   Yes.

Q   Where was he?

A   Over here in the county jail.

Q   How long had he been in the county jail, if
you know?

MR. FRINZI: Object to this as immaterial and
improper re-direct.

THE COURT: He may answer.

THE WITNESS: A Sometime in the late evening

63

hours the night before.

MR. SUTTON: Of the 16th?

A Yes.

Q All right. And, the weapon that you took from the Gein house was that a pistol or rifle?

A Hand gun.

Q Pistol?

A Yes.

MR. SUTTON: I have nothing further.

RE-CROSS EXAMINATION

BY

MR. FRINZI:

Q After you took this gun from the Gein home, did you at any time take it to Mr. Gein and ask him to identify it?

A No.

Q He never knew you took that gun from him then?

A Not that I know of.

MR. SUTTON: Object.

THE COURT: Sustained.

MR. SUTTON: That's all.

THE COURT: All right Mr. Murty, you can step down.

MR. FRINZI: I don't want to tie him up, but

GH

165

how far do you live from here?

                    (Discussion off the record.)

     THE COURT: We'll take a little break. The
Court will go read that law.

                    (Short recess taken.)

     THE COURT: All right.

     MR. FRINZI: Your Honor, may I be heard before
you make your ruling?

     THE COURT: Surely.

     MR. FRINZI: I had occasion to read these
three cases during the recess -- at least two of
them I scanned.

          The first two were 16 Wis. (2d) 241 and
the Case in 38 Wis. (2d) 392.

          So we get the record straight, 16 Wis. (2d)
241 and 38 Wis. (2d) 292.

          These are Civil cases. One case is an
automobile accident - a negligence case - and the
other case coming out of Kenosha County, Cossette
versus Lepp, involves a probate matter.

          The Case of State versus Smith is a Criminal
case. In that case the facts are not anywhere near
what the facts of this case are. In the Smith case
you have a situation where a home is in the process
of being burglarized -- the act itself is going on,

                                              65

your Honor --, and that is the reason that the rule is upheld in the Smith case - that the act is going on.

Now, here we got an act -- the defendant is charged with robbery and murder. The act is not going on. There is no relationship between the testimony here of Mr. Worden and the acts that are before the Court - the two charges. I'd like to make that distinction.

THE COURT: Well the Court has indicated that in a number of these cases that this matter of admitting such hearsay testimony is very discretionary with the Court.

In State versus Smith, 36 Wis. (2d) 584, page 594, the Court indicated two rules under which such statements might me admissible. Rule (a) is while the declarant was perceiving the event or condition which the statement narrates or describes or explains, immediately thereafter, and, (b) is the one that deals with the declarant being under the stress of nervous excitement, and so forth.

The Court thinks as to the statement made by Mr. Worden to Mr. Murty to the effect that something happened here -- "afraid something happened to Ma" -- that this is admissible under sub-section (a)

66

as something that was declared while the declarant was perceiving the event, or sufficiently close thereafter to be admissible.

As to the testimony relative to the asking to go roller skating and so forth, it seems to the Court pretty clear under Mr. Murty's testimony that this is something that Mr. Worden declared that apparently had been told to him, not something that he had observed. It gets too remote, and the Court will exclude that portion of the testimony, but the original statement as to, "I'm afraid something happened here," or, "afraid something happened to Ma," will be admitted.

Call your next witness.

MR. SUTTON: Captain Lloyd Schoephoester.

CAPTAIN LLOYD SCHOEPHOESTER, called as a witness herein, having been first duly sworn, was examined and testified as follows:

DIRECT EXAMINATION

BY

MR. SUTTON:

Q What is your name?

A Lloyd Schoephoester.

Q Where do you live Mr. Schoephoester?

A Markesan.

67

Q What is your occupation?

A Captain, Greenlake County Police.

Q How long have you been employed by the Greenlake County Police Department?

A Twenty years.

Q You were so employed on November 16, 1957?

A Yes.

Q I direct your attention to that date, did you have occasion to come to Waushara County?

A I did.

Q Would you describe approximately what time you came to Waushara County?

A I arrived at 7:25 at Plainfield.

Q And where did you proceed?

A I went to Worden's Store where I met Sheriff Schley.

Q And how long did you stay at the Worden store?

A Just a short time.

Q Then where did you proceed?

A We then went to Gein's farm.

Q By "we", who do you mean?

A Sheriff Schley and myself. He accompanied me.

Q And did you drive, or did he?

68

A   I drove.

Q   Approximately what time did you arrive at the Gein Farm?

A   About 8:00 P.M.

Q   Would you describe what transpired when you arrived there?

A   When we got there we went into a side door which apparently was a woodshed, and we found a body in there.

Q   Would you describe the condition that body was in, if you could?

MR. FRINZI: Just a minute. If the Court please, although the Court ruled on the matter of suppression of evidence by way of motion before the trial, to preserve the record, I'd like to have a continuing objection of the same grounds, that it's the contention of the defendant that the search and seizure here was illegal. And I'd like to have that in the record, your Honor, despite the fact that the Court has ruled by way of motion.

THE COURT: It will be so understood.

Was there a pending question, Mr. Brillowski?

COURT REPORTER: Yes, sir.

MR. SUTTON:Q Describe the condition of the

69

body as you recall it to the best of your ability?

THE WITNESS: A Well, the body was hanging in this woodshed by the ankles, and there was -- the tendons of the ankles were cut, and a rod put through there, and it was pulled up with a block and tackle.

MR. FRINZI: Could you speak a little louder?

THE WITNESS: A The body was in this woodshed, and there was -- the tendons had been cut in the ankle, a rod put through there and the body was lifted up with a block and tackle so the feet were near the ceiling, and the body was dressed out, and the head was missing.

Q Could you tell whether it was a male or female body?

A Yes. It was a female.

MR. SUTTON: Please mark these?

    (Whereupon, said documents were marked Plaintiff's Exhibits Nos. 4, 5, 6, 7 & 8 for Identification.)

I show you what has been marked as State's Exhibit No. 1 for Identification and ask you what that is?

THE WITNESS: A That's Gein's home, where we

70

found the body.

Q It's a photograph, is it not?

A Yes.

Q What is it a photograph of?

A Gein's farm.

Q Does it accurately depict the farm as you recall it on November 16, 1957?

A Yes, sir.

Q And do you know in what county that farm was?

A Waushara County.

Q I show you what has been marked State's Exhibit No. 2 for Identification, and ask what that is?

A Photograph.

Q And that's a photograph of --

A The Gein Farm.

Q And I show you what has been marked State's Exhibit No. 3 for Identification, and ask what that is?

A It's a photograph also.

Q What is that a photograph of?

A Back part of the Gein Home.

Q Do State's Exhibits Nos. 1, 2 & 3 accurately depict the farm as you recall it on November 16, 1957?

A Yes, sir.

71

Q   I show you what has been marked State's Exhibit No. 4 for Identification --

MR. FRINZI: Object to any questions on these pictures unless they relate to the cause of death.

MR. SUTTON: I know of no authority for that position.

THE COURT: I don't either.

MR. FRINZI: Pardon?

THE COURT: What authority do you have for that?

MR. FRINZI: It's basic under the rules of evidence. I don't think there's any authority needed here. Unless these pictures relate to the cause of death, their immaterial and irrelevant, your Honor.

THE COURT: Objection overruled.

MR. SUTTON: Q   I show you what has been marked State's Exhibit No. 4, and ask you what it is?

A   A photograph.

Q   What is that a photograph of, Captain?

MR. FRINZI: Excuse me, Judge, I make another objection, and offer another reason. It's duplicitus. He already described the condition of the body, and all these pictures do -- it's just a photograph of what he said in words of his prior testimony. It's

72

duplicitus. He testified as to the condition he found that body.

THE COURT: Overruled. You may answer.

MR. SUTTON: Q What is that a photograph of?

A Of the body of Mrs. Worden.

Q Does that photograph accurately depict the body you observed on the Gein farm on November 16, 1957?

A Yes, sir.

Q Was the body in that condition when you first observed it?

A Yes.

Q By that I mean in that physical condition, hanging as depicted there.

A Yes.

MR. FRINZI: Object as leading and suggestive, your Honor. The picture speaks for itself. He's leading him. I object, your Honor, on the grounds that the question was leading and suggestive.

THE COURT: He may answer.

MR. SUTTON: I beleive he already answered.

Now, I show you State's Exhibit No. 5 for Identification, and ask you what that is?

A A photograph also.

Q What is that a photograph of?

73

174

A   Of the body of Mrs. Worden.

Q   Does that photograph accurately depict the body that you observed on the Gein farm on November 16, 1957?

A   Yes, sir.

MR. FRINZI: Objected to as leading and suggestive.

THE COURT: He may answer, and the answer may stand. When there is an objection, Captain, don't answer until I rule, please.

MR. SUTTON: Q   I show you what has been marked State's Exhibit No. 6 for Identification, and ask you what that is?

A   A photograph.

Q   What is that a photograph of?

A   Of the body of Mrs. Worden.

Q   Does that photograph accurately depict the body you observed on the Gein farm on November 16, 1957?

MR. FRINZI: Object on the same grounds. Leading and suggestive.

THE COURT: He may answer.

THE WITNESS: A Yes, it is.

MR. SUTTON: Q   I show you what has been marked State's Exhibit No. 7 for Identification and ask you what that is?

74

A   Also a photograph.

Q   What is that a photograph of?

A   Mrs. Worden's body.

Q   Does that photograph accurately depict the body you observed in the Gein farm on November 16, 1957?

MR. FRINZI: Objected to on the same grounds, leading and suggestive.

THE COURT: He may answer.

THE WITNESS: A Yes, it is.

MR. SUTTON: I show you what has been marked State's Exhibit No. 8 for Identification and ask you what that is?

A   Also a photograph.

Q   What is that a photograph of?

A   Of Mrs. Worden's body.

Q   Does that photograph accurately depict the body as you observed it on the Gein farm on November 16, 1957?

MR. FRINZI: Object. Leading and suggestive.

THE COURT: He may answer.

THE WITNESS: A Yes, it is.

MR. SUTTON: Q Now, Captain Schoephoester, after you and Sheriff Schley discovered the body, what did you do?

75

A Then we contacted Officer Chase - Deputy
Chase - and asked him if he still had Mr. Gein
in his custody.

MR. SUTTON: Your witness.

CROSS EXAMINATION

BY

MR. FRINZI:

Q Now, what time did you say you came into
Plainfield, Captain?

A 7:25.

Q Where did you first go when you came into
Plainfield?

A I went directly to the Worden Hardware Store.

Q Did you go directly into the Hardware Store?

A I did not. I did not leave my car.

Q You met Sheriff Schley outside?

A Yes. He came to the car.

Q I see. And, where did you go from the
outside the Worden Hardware Store with Sheriff
Schley?

A Went directly to the Gein home.

Q Just the two of you?

A Yes, sir.

Q You and the Sheriff?

A Yes, sir.

76

Q What if anything did you do after you approached the Gein Farm?

A Well, we drove in the car, and then went directly into the woodshed.

Q Was there a door there?

A Yes.

Q And did you knock on the door?

A No, sir.

Q Just walked in?

A Yes, sir.

Q You didn't have permission or consent from Ed Gein to go in there, did you?

A No.

Q Did you have a search warrant or any other process to go into the premises of Ed Gein?

MR. SUTTON: Object to this line of questioning. This question already has been resolved.

THE COURT: The Court will permit it for purposes of building a record.

MR. SUTTON: Alright.

THE COURT: Did he answer?

THE WITNESS: A I did not have a search warrant, no.

MR. FRINZI: Q You don't know whether Sheriff Schley had a search warrant, do you?

77

A   I do not know.

Q   Did you know Mrs. Worden prior to the night of November 16, 1957?

A   No, sir.

Q   Did you ever see her before?

A   No, sir.

Q   You didn't know whose body this was from your own personal knowledge?

A   To my own personal knowledge, no.

Q   Now, did you find any firearms in the residence of Edward Gein?

A   I did not, no.

Q   Did you see any firearms?

A   Yes, I did.

Q   What if any firearms did you see in the residence?

A   .32 calibre revolver.

Q   You didn't touch it?

A   No.

Q   But you saw it?

A   Yes.

Q   Did you see a cash register in the Gein house?

A   Yes.

Q   With respect to the cash register, did you

78

179

notice whether there was anything in the cash register?

A There wasn't, no.

Q Pardon?

A There wasn't anything in the cash register. It had been broken open.

MR. FRINZI: I move that that be stricken as a conclusion on his part. That was not the question.

THE COURT: The "broken" part will be stricken. He can testify whether or not it was open.

THE WITNESS: A Yes, it was.

MR. FRINZI: Q Now, how long -- excuse me. How long were you in the Gein residence when you went in there the first time with Sheriff Schley?

A Well, I don't know exactly. I was in and out of the building.

Q The first time you went in, how long were you in there?

A Just momentarily.

Q And then you left the building?

A Yes.

Q And how soon after did you go back in?

A Well, after I made some calls on the radio I then went back into the building.

Q How long were you in there the second time

79

you went back into the building?

A Possibly an hour.

Q And who was with you at that time when you went back the second time into the Gein residence?

A Sheriff Schley.

Q Just the two of you?

A Yes.

Q No other deputies or officers?

A Not at that time.

Q After you remained there an hour, where did you go from there?

A I had gone back into Wautoma one time.

Q Did you return to the Gein farm any more that night?

A Yes.

Q What time abut?

A It's hard to remember. It would be before mid-night, I'm sure.

Q Who did you go back there with the third time?

A I was by myself.

Q Alone?

A Yes.

Q Was there someone there when you arrived at the Gein residence?

Ro

A   Yes.

Q   Now, from the time that you left -- you had been there the second time and then you left, and to the time you got back, you don't know who, if anybody, was there, do you?

A   No, sir.

Q   Now, was the area barricaded to your knowledge?

A   Yes, it was.

Q   What do you mean by barricaded?

A   Well, Sheriff Schley had stationed deputies around the area.

Q   You don't know to your own knowledge whether these deputies were there all the time?

MR. SUTTON: Object.   Argumentative.

MR. FRINZI: This is cross examination.

THE COURT: Obviously he wouldn't know if he wasn't there.   Objection sustained.

MR. FRINZI: Q   Well, there were barricades put up?

THE WITNESS: A   No barricades, no sir.

Q   You don't know who, if anybody, guarded this Gein residence, do you?

A   I know some of the officers, not too many.

Q   You don't know if it was under guard all

81

the time, do you?

A   As far as I know, it was.

Q   Were you there all the time?

MR. SUTTON: Object.   He's arguing with the witness.

THE COURT: Obviously.

MR. FRINZI: I'll withdraw the question.

Were you present at all times at the Gein residence?

A   No, sir.

Q   You don't know who, if anybody was there al during the night, do you?

A   No, sir.

Q   Now, did you go back in there - into the Ge residence the third time you went back?

A   Yes, sir.

Q   With whom did you go in there with?

A   I went in with -- by myself.

Q   Who was there when you got there?

A   Sheriff Schley, Sheriff Wanserski from Portage County, Officer Neilson from Marquette County and Deputy Murty, Deputy Fritz, and I think the Crime Lab was there.   There were others who I didn't know - other officers.

82

Q What happened to the premises from the time
you left, after you had gone in the second time, to
the third time, you don't know?

A In the meantime?

Q You don't know what happened because you
were gone.

A No.

Q So you don't know what happened then?

A No.

Q Now, did you have occasion to see or observe
any bullets in the Gein home?

A No, I did not.

Q Just observed the gun?

A Pardon?

Q You observed the gun?

A Yes.

Q No bullets?

A No bullets.

MR. FRINZI: That's all.

MR. SUTTON: That's all.

THE COURT: That's all, Captain.

    You want him to stay?

MR. FRINZI: He's down at Greenlake. We can
get him shortly.

    (Off the record.)

THE COURT: Are you on duty this week, or what?

83

184

THE WITNESS: In our department as small as it is, were always on duty.

THE COURT: Off the record.

(Discussion off the record.)

Next witness.

MR. SUTTON: Mr. Allan Wilimovsky.

THE COURT: He's back in the back room.

ALLAN WILIMOVSKY

called as a witness herein, having been first duly sworn, was examined and testified as follows:

DIRECT EXAMINATION

BY

MR. SUTTON:

Q What is your name?

A Allan E. Wilimovsky.

Q And your occupation?

A I'm a Firearms Identification Specialist, Wisconsin Department of Justice, Crime Laboratory Division.

Q And approximately how long have you been employed by the State Crime Laboratory?

A Approximately nineteen and a half years.

Q Were you so employed then on November 16, 1957?

A I was.

84

Q   Did you have occasion that day to come to Waushara County?

A   I did.

Q   Where was the State Crime Laboratory located on November 16, 1957?

A   907 University Avenue, Madison, Wisconsin.

Q   And on November 16, 1957, did you have occasion to come to Waushara County?

A   I did.

Q   And approximately what time?

A   Late evening, approximately 10 or 10:30 that evening, 16th of November.

Q   And, who, if anyone, was with you?

A   Mr. Jan Beck of the Laboratory Staff and Mr. James Halligan, also of the Laboratory Staff.

Q   And, by what mode of transportation?

MR. FRINZI: Hold it. I'd like to get the first names.

THE WITNESS: Jan, J-A-N, the last name is Beck, B-E-C-K.

MR. SUTTON: Man or woman?

A   A man.

Q   What was the second one?

A   James Halligan.

85

Q   How do you spell it?

A   H-a-l-l-i-g-a-n.   I'm not sure of that, but I beleive that's the spelling.

Q   What mode of transportation -- by what mode of transportation did you come from Madison to Waushara County?

A   We were in the Crime Laboratory's Mobile Field Unit.

Q   When you arrived in Waushara County approximately 10:00 or 10:30 in the evening, where did you proceed?

A   We were escorted to a dwelling which was located southwest of Plainfield, Wisconsin.

Q   When you got to that dwelling, what if anything did you do?

A   Mr. Beck and Mr. Halligan, and myself, along with three other officers, entered the dwelling.

Q   What if anything did you find in the dwelling?

A   I observed a body.

Q   Could you describe the condition of that body?

A   Yes.   This body was suspended --

MR. FRINZI: Object to that, your Honor.   It's duplicitus.   He already had the last witness describe the condition of that body.

86

187

THE COURT: No. He may answer.

MR. SUTTON: Go ahead. You may answer.

THE WITNESS: A I observed a body which was suspended by a short length of wooden pole suspended from the ankles, being supported by the ceiling rafters of this particular area.

Q Did you have occasion that evening to photograph that body?

A I did.

Q Now, I show you what has been marked State's Exhibit No. 4 for Identification, and ask you what that is?

A Exhibit 4 is a photographic print of a picture that I took of the body that I observed at that particular dwelling at that time.

Q Does that accurately depict what you observed when you took the photograph?

A It does.

Q There is some information on the back of that photograph. What does that information reflect?

A This information reflects the size and type of camera, the lens, the exposure, the type of film used, the direction in which the camera was pointed, and approximate distance between the camera and the subject.

87

Q   I show you what has been marked State's
Exhibit No. 5 for Identification and ask you
what that is?

A   This is a print of a photograph that I
took of the body which I observed at that particular dwelling on November 16, 1957. These were
taken the early morning of the 17th of November.

Q   Does Exhibit 5 accurately depict what you
observed when you took the photographs?

A   It does.

Q   And does the reverse side of Exhibit 5
contain the same information relative to the
camera, etc., that was contained on Exhbit 4?

MR. FRINZI: We'll save alot of time:
As far as those Exhibits are concerned I will
stipulate to the accuracy of those Exhibits, but
not to the materiality, and then you can save
alot of time asking him the same questions and
getting the same answers.

THE COURT: You will stipulate as to the
technical data contained in the back?

MR. FRINZI: To the accuracy.

THE COURT: Alright.

MR. SUTTON: At this time the State would
offer into evidence State's Exhibits Nos. 4, 5,

88

189

6, 7, and 8.

MR. FRINZI: Object as to materiality.

THE COURT: Exhibits 4 thru 8 are received.
Do you have them?

THE WITNESS: Yes, right here.

(Whereupon, Plaintiff's Exhibit
Nos. 4, 5, 6, 7 & 8 for
Identification were received
in evidence.)

MR. FRINZI: Have you concluded your direct
examination of this witness, Mr. Sutton?

MR. SUTTON: No, I haven't.

Q   Now, I show you what has been marked
State's Exhibit No. 2 and 3 --

MR. FRINZI: Again I'll stipulate before you
go further -- to save a little time here -- I'll
stipulate to the accuracy of those pictures, but
not to the materiality.

THE COURT: Alright. Were they taken by
Mr. Wilimovsky?

MR. SUTTON: No, these three photographs
were taken by another witness.

MR. FRINZI: Let's get off the record a
minute. Is he around?

MR. SUTTON: No, let's stay on the record.

89

Yes, he's around.

MR. FRINZI: We'll stipulate to the accuracy.

MR. SUTTON: Q I show you State's Exhibit No. 1 for Identification, and ask you what it is?

THE WITNESS: A Exhibit No. 1 is a photographic print of a photograph which was taken of the dwelling.

Q Now, let me ask you, Mr. Wilimovsky: does that accurately depict the dwelling you testified to where you discovered the body, or where you observed this body?

A Yes.

Q I show you State's Exhibit No. 2 marked for Identification and ask you what that is?

A This is also a photograph of the same building.

Q The dwelling wherein you observed the body you testified to?

MR. FRINZI: Hold it. Object on the grounds that it's leading the witness.

MR. SUTTON: He may tell whether or not it's the building in which he observed the body he testified to.

THE WITNESS: A It is.

90

191

MR. FRINZI: Leading and suggestive, your Honor.

THE COURT: He may answer.

THE WITNESS: A This is the dwelling, yes.

MR. SUTTON: Q I show you what has been marked State's Exhibit No. 3 for Identification and ask what that is?

A This is a photograph of the dwelling in which I observed the body on November 16, 1957.

MR. SUTTON: I understand you stipulate to the method that the photograph was taken?

MR. FRINZI: I stipulate to the accuracy, but not to the materiality.

MR. SUTTON: At this time I offer what have been marked as State's Exhibits Nos. 1, 2, and 3 for Identification.

THE COURT: Exhibits 1, 2 and 3 are received.

(Whereupon, Plaintiff's Exhibits Nos. 1, 2, and 3 for Identification were received in evidence.)

MR. SUTTON: Q Now, Mr. Wilimovsky, would you describe what if anything was done with the body after you took the photographs?

MR. FRINZI: Object to that. That's not

91

within the personal knowledge of this witness.

MR. SUTTON: If it's within your personal knowledge.

THE COURT: I don't know whether it is or not. You better back up Mr. Sutton and find out.

MR. FRINZI: He's putting the cart before the horse.

MR. SUTTON: Q Do you know what happened to the body?

A I do.

Q Would you tell us, please.

A After I photographed the body, the body was released to Mr. Ray Goult, of the Goult Funeral Home, Plainfield, Wisconsin.

Q Did you see the body again that morning.

A Late morning, early afternoon of the 17th, which I beleive was Sunday.

Q Where did you see that body?

A Goult Funeral Home, Plainfield, Wisconsin.

Q What if anything occurred there in your presence?

A A post mortem examination of the body was conducted.

Q Now, going back to the dwelling within which you observed the body, would you tell us,

92

did you make a search of that area.

A Yes.

Q What if anything else did you discover?

A Many things.

Q Did you discover anything that was connected in any way with the body?

A I did.

MR. FRINZI: We object to that. It's immaterial.

THE COURT: I don't know whether it is or not. I don't know what he's going to say. He may answer.

THE WITNESS: A I did.

MR. SUTTON: Q What was that?

A I found a human head.

Q And where did you find the human head?

A In very close proximity to where the body was found.

Q Did you have occasion to photograph that head?

A I did.

MR. SUTTON: Mark these please?

                    (Whereupon, said photographs
                    were marked Plaintiff's Exhibits
                    Nos. 9, 10 & 11 for Identifica-
                    tion.)

MR. FRINZI: Will you stipulate to the accuracy

93

of these Exhibits?

MR. FRINZI: No, I'm not going to stipulate to these unless you got something to show me. These are just prints. There is nothing here about lens or anything.

MR. SUTTON: Q I show you what has been marked Exhibit No. 9 and ask you what it is?

THE WITNESS: A Exhibit 9 is a photograph which I took of the right side of the head.

Q Does that accurately depict -- did you take that photograph?

A This was taken on the 17th of November, 1957, while at the Goult Funeral Home.

Q Does that accurately depict the head as you saw it at the time you photographed it?

MR. FRINZI: Object to/proper foundation
                    no
having been laid here.

THE COURT: He may answer.

THE WITNESS: A It does.

MR. SUTTON: Q I show you what has been marked State's Exhibit No. 10 for Identification and ask you what that is?

A This is a photograph which I took of the left side of the head on November 17, 1957, while

94

at the Goult Funeral Home in Plainfield, Wisconsin.

Q Does that accurately depict the head as
you observed it on that day?

A It does.

Q I show you what has been marked Exhibit 11
for Identification and ask you what that is?

A States Exhibit No. 11 is a photograph
which I took showing a frontal view or a face
view of the head on November 17, 1957, while at
the Goult Funeral Home in Plainfield, Wisconsin.

Q Does that accurately depict the head you
observed at the time you took the photograph.

A It does.

MR. SUTTON: At this time, your Honor, the
State would offer into evidence what have been
marked State's Exhibits Nos. 9, 10, and 11 for
Identification as State's Exhibits 9, 10 & 11.

MR. FRINZI: At this time the Defense objects
to these Exhibits on the ground that proper authenticit
has not been established.

MR. SUTTON: Under the statutes, I beleive, if
Mr. Frinzi is objecting to the fact that these
photographs do not have the information on the
reverse side as the others, I beleive under the
statute, that is not an absolute requirement, and

95

he has a right to cross examine with regard why that information isn't there.

Unless you want me to bring it out.

THE COURT: Alright, go ahead.

MR. SUTTON: Q Mr. Wilimovsky, why are there no indications on the reverse sides of Exhibits 9, 10 and 11 regarding the type of camera and distance from the object, etc.?

THE WITNESS: A Apparently it was not recorded.

Q At the time?

A That's correct.

MR. SUTTON: I make the offer, subject to the statute.

MR. FRINZI: I renew my objection. I have a right to cross examine on that also.

THE COURT: That's right. You want to do it -- let's do it this way: The Court will reserve ruling on Exhibits 9 10 and 11 until after Mr. Frinzi completes his cross examination.

We will take a recess at this time until 1:30.

(Witness temporarily excused.)

(Which were all the proceedings

96

had in this cause at this
session, and this matter was
continued to 1:30 o'clock p.m.
this date.)

97

STATE OF WISCONSIN   )
)   SS:
COUNTY OF WAUSHARA   )

      IN THE CIRCUIT COURT OF WAUSHARA COUNTY

STATE OF WISCONSIN,   )
)
            Plaintiff,   )
)
      vs.   )   No.
)
EDWARD GEIN,   )
)
            Defendant.   )

                  Thursday, November 7, 1968

                  1:30 o'clock p.m.

BEFORE: The Honorable ROBERT H. GOLLMAR

    Court met pursuant to adjournment.

APPEARANCES:

    Same as before.

ALLAN WILIMOVSKY,

recalled to the stand, having been previously duly
sworn, on oath was further examined and testified
as follows:

DIRECT EXAMINATION (cont'd.)

BY

MR. SUTTON:

Q Now, Mr. Wilimovsky, before I continue
with the testimony you were giving as to what
transpired at the premises, I would like to ask
you a few more questions with regard to State's
Exhibits 9, 10 and 11.

Do you recall what kind of camera you
used to take those photographs?

A I do.

Q What kind was it?

A Four inch by five inch Speed Graphic camera.

Q Is that the same camera you took the other
photographs that have already been admitted in
evidence?

A Yes.

MR. SUTTON: At this time I offer State's
Exhibits 9, 10 and 11.

MR. FRINZI: At this time I ask the Court to
reserve it's ruling until we had an opportunity to
cross examine the witness.   99

THE COURT: Very well.

MR. SUTTON: Q Now, Mr. Wilimovsky, after you discovered the head at the dwelling, what if anything did you do with the head?

A The head was photographed, and then it was released.

Q And were you present when it was released?

A I was.

Q And who was it released to?

A It is my recollection that it was Deputy Sheriff Chase, but I'm not completely positive on that point. It was a Waushara County Deputy Sheriff.

Q Did you have occasion to see the body and the head again on the morning of the 17th of November, 1957?

A Late morning of the 17th, yes.

Q And where did you see the body and the head?

A This was at the Goult Funeral Home, Plainfield Wisconsin.

Q And what transpired at that time?

A At that time a post mortem was made.

Q And who conducted that post mortem examination?

A Doctor Eigenberger from Sheboygan, Wisconsin.

100

201

Q Were you present?

A I was.

Q Who else was present?

A Mrs. Eigenberger, Mr. James Halligan of the Laboratory staff, and if my memory serves me correctly, the Sheriff of Sheboygan County, and a Deputy Sheriff of Sheboygan County.

Q Do you know Mrs. Eigenberger?

A I do.

Q Would you tell us whether or not she was present?

A She was.

Q Approximately how long did that take, or how long were you there?

A It was very late afternoon of the 17th when the post mortum examination was completed at the Goult Funeral Home.

Q Now, did you have occasion to see the head on other premises that day.

A I did.

Q Where was that?

A The head was transported from the Goult Funeral Home in Plainfield, Wisconsin, to the Coroners office at Wautoma, Wisconsin.

Q And were you present in the Coroners office

EO1

A   I was.

Q   And who was present there besides yourself?

A   Doctor Eigenberger, Mrs. Eigenberger, Mr. Jim Halligan, myself, and there may have been other people, but I don't recall.

Q   What occurred at that time at those premises?

A   The head was X-Rayed.

Q   And after the head was X-Rayed, what if anything was done?

A   A bullet was subsequently recovered from the head.

Q   And how was the bullet recovered from the head?

A   The bullet was recovered from the head by Doctor Eigenberger.

Q   Were you present when that was done?

A   I was.

Q   And what operation if any, did he perform to recover the bullet?

A   The skull cap was removed, and dissection was accomplished which led to the retrieval of the bullet.

Q   And what did Doctor Eigenberger do with that bullet when he recovered it?

A   He handed it to me.

102

MR. SUTTON: At this time your Honor I would like to turn Mr. Wilimovsky over to Mr. Frinzi for cross examination, after which I would like him to step down to be recalled later for further testimony.

THE COURT: Alright. Go ahead Mr. Frinzi.

CROSS EXAMINATION

BY

MR. FRINZI:

Q Now, your a member of the present Department of Justice, Criminal Division, is that correct?

A Department of Justice, Crime Laboratory Division.

Q But in 1957 that was known as the Crime Lab. of the State of Wisconsin, right?

A Yes, the Wisconsin State Crime Laboratory.

Q Now, what time did you get to the Gein home on the night of November 16, 1957?

A It's my recollection that it was about 10:30 or 11:00 o'clock p.m., Saturday night.

Q I see. Now, did you have occasion on the night of November 16, or the day of November 17, 1957 to go to the Worden Hardware Store?

A Not on those dates, no, sir.

103

Q Well, did you at any time subsequent to November 16, 1957, go to the Worden Hardware Store?

A I did.

Q What day?

MR. SUTTON: Object, your Honor. This is beyond the scope of the direct examination. I'll elicit testimony on the same matter when I put Mr. Wilimovsky on the stand at a later time in the case.

THE COURT: Alright.

MR. FRINZI: I'll withdraw the question then.

THE COURT: It will be understood you will have a further right of cross examination.

MR. FRINZI: I will withdraw the last question if that is Mr. Sutton's intention, your Honor.

Now, you went onto the premises of Edward Gein on the night of November 16, 1957?

THE WITNESS: A I did.

Q And did you have the consent or permission of Mr. Edward Gein to go onto the premises?

A I did not.

Q Did you have a search warrant at the time you entered the premises of Edward Gein?

A I did not.

Q Did you go on the premises alone or with

104

someone else?

A With someone else. .

Q Who was that somebody else?

A Mr. James Halligan and Jan Beck of the
Laboratory Staff, Deputy Sheriff David Sharkey of
theWood County Sheriff's office, Deputy Arnold
Fritz of the Waushara County office, and -- I'm
not sure I'm pronouncing it properly -- Captain
Schoephoester of Greenlake County Sheriff's office.

Q To your knowledge, did any of these people
that went onto the premises with you have a search
warrant for the search of the premises of Edward
Gein?

MR. SUTTON: Object to this inquiry, your Honor,
this has been resolved in this case.

THE COURT: The Court ruled before that he could
go into this simply for the purpose of establishing
the record.

He may answer.

THE WITNESS: A If they did, I was unaware of
it.

MR. FRINZI: To your knowledge, you didn't know
if any of them had a search warrant?

A That is true.

Q Now, did you take any item from the

105

premises of Edward Gein on either the night of
November 16, 1957, or November 17, 1957?

A I did.

Q Did you take a gun from the premises?

A Yes. I beleive on the 17th.

Q You did take a gun?

A Yes.

Q And how did you take that gun? How did you
go about taking the gun from the premises?

A I physically took the firearm from the
premises and carried it out to the mobile field
unit and locked it in the field unit.

Q Now, what kind of gun was that?

A There were several.

Q Well, how many did you take?

A I don't beleive that I can answer that
definitively. There were several firearms. There
were several people recovering these items.

Q My question is, Mr. Wilimovsky, how many
firearms did you take from the premises of
Edward Gein?

A I have a recollection of one specific
firearm..

Q Do you know what type of firearm that was?

A I do.

Q What type?

106

A German manufactured 1910 Model Mauser,
.32 automatic pistol calibre. It was contained in
a black leather holster. The firearm was loaded.

Q Now, did you consider that a deadly weapon?

MR. SUTTON: Object. Immaterial.

THE COURT: He may answer.

THE WITNESS: A It could have been considered
such a weapon, yes.

MR. FRINZI: Q A deadly weapon?

MR. SUTTON: That's repetitive.

MR. FRINZI: He answered. I'll withdraw that
part.

Did you have occasion to observe any
other firearms on the premises of Edward Gein?

A I did.

Q What type of firearms were the others that
you observed?

A They consisted of shoulder guns, rifles,
and shot guns, and one .22 calibre revolver.

Q How many to the best of your recollection --
how many firearms would you say were on the premises
of Edward Gein that you observed?

A Hazarding a guess, possibly half a dozen.

Q Were these other firearms that you just

107

described taken from the premises of Edward Gein?

A They were.

Q And you don't know who took the others, other than the one that you took?

A I could have taken some of the others. I don't recall.

Q Would you describe to the Court the procedure that you used in taking these firearms from the premises?

A I don't recall that I specifically removed the shoulder guns from the premises, but it has been my procedure --

Q I don't want to know what your procedure is. What did you do on this particular occasion in removing the particular firearm that you said you removed from the premises?

A This one I just physically picked up and took out to the mobile unit.

Q You didn't use any handkerchief?

A No. I held the firearm by the holster it was contained in.

Q To your knowledge, do you know whether or not you touched that firearm at all?

A I probably did.

108

Q   Do you know if anyone else prior to your
coming in there touched that firearm or any other
firearm that was in the Gein home?

A   I don't know.

Q   Did you at any time confront Mr. Gein
with this firearm or any other firearm?

A   In what way?

Q   Well, did you show him the firearm and ask
him if it was his gun?

A   I did not.

Q   Did you have occasion to observe whether
or not there were any bullets in the home of
Edward Gein?

A   Yes.

Q   And would you tell the Court what if anything you observed with respect to bullets in the
home of Edward Gein?

A   I observed one .32 calibre automatic pistol
bullet which was a fired bullet that had a small
wire loop attached to its base.

I observed two boxes of .22 calibre
cartridges, and one partial box as I recall, of
12 guage shotgun shells.

Q   Now, did you remove any of those bullets
from the home of Edward Gein?

109

A   I removed the bullets and the boxes of ammunition, yes.

Q   When you removed them, was there anyone else present at the time you removed the bullets?

A   I don't recall.

Q   Did you make any markings on the bullets when you removed them from the home of Edward Gein?

A   No, not at that time.

Q   Now, incidently, when you removed the gun from the home of Edward Gein, prior to removing it from the home, did you put any markings on the gun prior to your removing it to the mobile unit?

A   I did not.

Q   Do you know where these bullets are now that you removed from the home of Edward Gein?

A   I do.

Q   Where are they?

A   In Madison.

Q   Are they still there now?

A   Yes.

Q   Where are they in Madison?

A   They're locked in the gun room vault.

Q   Now, you didn't know Mrs. Bernice Worden, did you?

A   No, I did not.

110

Q So you didn't know who Bernice Worden was,
is that right?

A That's true.

Q Of your own personal knowledge.

A Correct.

Q Now, did you have occasion to observe a
cash register on the premises of Edward Gein?

A I don't recall. I did see a cash register,
but I don't recall if I saw it contained within the
premises or outside of the premises.

Q I see. And, you don't know of your own
personal knowledge whether that cash register was
the property of Bernice Worden, did you?

A I do not.

Q Now, did you have occasion to examine this
cash register at any time on the premises?

A I did not.

Q Now you testified that you were, I beleive,
if my memory serves me correctly, on November 17,
at a funeral home in Plainfield, is that correct?

A Yes.

Q Would you tell me the name of that funeral
home?

A Goult's Funeral Home.

111

Q I beleive you said you were present at the time Doctor Eigenberger, along with other people, conducted a post mortem examination of the body that was in the funeral home?

A Yes.

Q And did you have occasion to observe what the other people were doing there?

A Well, Doctor Eigenberger --

Q Just answer. Did you have occasion --

A Yes.

Q Did you have occasion to observe what the other people that were there doing?

A Not all of the people, no.

Q Now, I beleive you testified Mr. Halligan was there?

A Yes.

Q Did you have occasion to observe what he was doing -- I'll make it easier. I'll rephrase the question.

Did you have occasion to observe Mr. Halligan from time to time while he was in the funeral home while that post mortem examination was being conducted?

A Yes, I did.

Q What if anything do you remember off and on

112

as to what Mr. Halligan was doing?

A I can't recall anything specific.

Q Was he just observing?

A Observing and assisting in anyway that
he could.

Q In what way was he assisting, if you know?

A I don't recall.

Q Now, I beleive you said that Doctor
Eigenberger removed a bullet lodged in the head
that was at the funeral home?

A Yes.

Q And he turned that bullet over to you?

A Yes.

Q At the time he turned that bullet over to
you, do you recall whether he or you made any specific
markings on that bullet?

A I did.

Q What if anything did you mark on that
bullet?

A I inscribed my initials on the base portion
of the bullet.

Q Were there any other markings that you put
on that bullet?

A Yes, the file in which it was contained was
marked by Doctor Eigenberger and myself.

113

Q I am talking about the bullet itself.

A Any other markings?

Q Yes.

A Yes.

Q What other markings were put on the bullet other than your initials?

A Yes.

Q What were they?

A An Exhibit designation and Case number.

Q On the bullet?

A Yes.

Q Your talking about taking a piece of paper and taping it on there and inscribed on the bullet?

A They were inscribed.

Q Where is that bullet?

A In my possession.

Q Where is it.

A In my pocket.

MR. FRINZI: Your Honor, at this time I am going to make a demand on the State that I be given an opportunity at some time during the course of this trial to have an individual from the Defense examine that particular bullet.

THE COURT: Do you have such an expert here?

MR. FRINZI: Not today, but I will have one before this trial is concluded.

114

THE COURT: Well, the Court sees no reason why your expert should not examine it under proper safe guard, presumably in the presence of Mr. Wilimovsky.

Do you have any question on that, Mr. Sutton.

MR. SUTTON: I have no objection. I think it's somewhat premature. I prefer he did it after the second time Mr. Wilimovsky is on the stand and all the evidence on the bullet is all in.

THE COURT: That may well be, but that's a matter of effect. I suppose Mr. Frinzi has notified his expert to come up here. I don't assume he's here in Wautoma.

I'm going to permit it.

MR. SUTTON: I have no objection to it.

THE COURT: All right, it will be so understood.

MR. FRINZI: Q Who else was there besides you, Doctor Eigenberger, Mr. Halligan, and Mrs. Eigenberger?

THE WITNESS: A The persons that I recall being present were Doctor Eigenberger, Mrs. Eigenberger, Mr. Jim Halligan, Mr. Ray Goult was there, and myself, and if my memory serves me correctly, I beleive the sheriff and deputy sheriff from *Sheboygan County were also present.*

Q Do you recall seeing Mrs. Eigenberger? 115

216

A   I do.

Q   Do you recall, or did you make any observations as to what if anything she was doing?

A   I did.

Q   What did you observe?

A   She was seated in a chair taking notes which her husband was dictating.

Q   Now, did you observe whether she was taking these notes in the form of shorthand?

A   I did not notice.

Q   You don't know how she was taking these notes?

A   No, I don't.

Q   And you don't know if everything that the Doctor told her, whether she took all that down?

A   I do not.

Q   Do you know how fast the Doctor was talking as he was giving -- as he was making statements?

A   At the time I didn't pay any particular attention as to the rapidity in which he was speaking, no.

Q   You don't know whether he was going fast or slow?

A   I don't recall.

Q   You have no knowledge whether she took

116

every word down?

A I don't know.

Q You have no knowledge whether he told her what to take down and what to omit?

A I don't recall him making that statement.

MR. FRINZI: That's all for now. I understand from Mr. Sutton that Mr. Wilimovsky will be recalled.

MR. SUTTON: Yes, he will be back.

MR. FRINZI: All right.

MR. SUTTON: Mr. Wilimovsky, you may step down.

THE COURT: That's all for now.

MR. SUTTON: Deputy Chase.

THE COURT: Just a minute. You want him sequestered again from the court room?

MR. FRINZI: Yes, sir.

MR. SUTTON: I'd like to point something out: I have three exhibits that have been offered, and I anticipated Mr. Frinzi would use the opportunity to cross examine on those.

MR. FRINZI: I'm not going to cross examine.

THE COURT: All right, then Exhibits 9 through 11 are received.

(Whereupon, Plaintiff's Exhibits Nos. 9, 10, and 11 for Identification were received in evidence)

117

MR. SUTTON: Deputy Chase, please.

DAN CHASE,

called as a witness herein, having been first duly sworn, was examined and testified as follows:

DIRECT EXAMINATION

BY

MR. SUTTON:

Q What is your name?

A Dan Chase.

Q And what is your occupation?

A I'm retired at the present time.

Q What was your occupation in November of 1957?

A I was a County Traffic Officer, Waushara County.

Q Did you know the defendant, Edward Gein, before November 16, 1957?

A I did.

Q And approximately how long had you known him?

A Oh, three or four years before that time.

Q And did you know where Mr. Gein lived?

A I did.

Q I show you what have been marked and accepted in evidence as State's Exhibits 1, 2 and 3, and ask you what those are, Mr. Chase?

118

A   They're photos.

Q   What are they photographs of?

A   The Eddie Gein home - farm home.

Q   As it existed in November of 1957?

A   That's right.

Q   Did you know Mrs. Bernice Worden?

A   I did.

Q   And approximately how long had you known
Mrs. Bernice Worden on November 16, 1957?

A   Oh, at least ten years.

Q   I show you what are in evidence as State's
Exhibits 9, 10, and 11, and ask you to look at
those, please? What are those?

A   Photos.

Q   What are those photos of?

A   Of Mrs. Worden.

Q   Now, Mr. Chase, I direct your attention to
the early morning of November 17, 1957, did you
have occasion to be at Edward Gein's farm?

A   I was.

Q   Did you have occasion that morning to see
Mrs. Worden's head that is portrayed in the photographs?

A   I did.

Q   And what if anything did you do with that

119

head that morning?

A   I took it to the Goult Funeral Home at
Plainfield.

Q   And do you recall under whose supervision
you did that or who told you to go to take the head
to the Goult Funeral Home?

A   Mr. Wilimovsky, the gentleman that was just
on the witness stand.

Q   Allan Wilimovsky?

A   Allan Wilimovsky.

Q   And when you brought the head to the Goult
Funeral Home, what if anything did you do when you
got there?

A   I gave it to Raymond Goult.

Q   Did you have occasion to see the defendant,
Edward Gein, in the jail on the evening of November 16,
1957?

A   I did.

Q   And did you have occasion to see him without
his clothes on?

A   I did.

Q   Did you make any observations of his body
at that time?

A   I did.

Q   What if anything unusual did you notice?

120

221

A I noticed on his arm, high, that there was a spot on there that I beleived to be blood.

MR. SUTTON: Your witness.

CROSS EXAMINATION

BY

MR. FRINZI:

Q Now, your position at the time, November of 1957, was that of a county traffic officer?

A That's right.

Q I see. And were you on duty on that day?

A I was.

Q What time did you go on duty, Mr. Chase?

A That's hard to say. I was out from 2:00 in the morning, and then I was working right thru. I was to an accident out on 21 east of Redgranite, and then I came back to Wautoma, and I was going to go deer hunting, and I stopped to pick my clothes up, and I went deer hunting.

Q Now, you testified that you had occasion to see Ed Gein at the County Jail here in Waushara County - here in Wautoma - on the evening of November 16, 1957?

A That's right.

Q About what time was that Mr. Chase?

A Oh, as I recall, around 8:00.

Q Who, if anyone, was present at the time you saw Mr. Gein?

A Arden Spees.

Q Who is he? The sheriff?

A He's a deputy sheriff -- a deputy sheriff of Plainfield -- and I don't know if he was Marshall at that time or not.

Q Was Sheriff Schley there at that time?

A No.

Q Do you know whether or not Sheriff Schley had been there earlier at the County Jail?

A He was not.

Q Were you there all the while?

A I was there all the while.

Q Did you arrest Mr. Edward Gein?

A I did.

Q Where did you arrest him?

A In the Village of Plainfield.

Q What time did you arrest him?

A Somewhere around 7:30.

Q And you arrested him at the Hill Farm?

A No.

Q Where did you arrest him?

A Village of Plainfield.

THE COURT: That's 7:30 P.M. it's understood.

122

THE WITNESS: Yes.

MR. FRINZI: Q Did you go to the Hill Farm that night before you took Ed Gein into custody?

A I did.

Q Did you find Ed Gein at the Hill Farm?

A I did.

Q What if anything did you tell him at that time?

A I walked up to the car and saw him sitting in it, and asked him to come over and get in my car - that I wanted to talk to him.

Q And you say Deputy Spees was present with you?

A That's right.

Q And you took Ed Gein to the Sheriff's office in Wautoma, is that right?

A I didn't hear all the question.

Q I'm sorry. I'll have to speak a little louder.

Now, you took Ed Gein to the Sheriff's office - to the County Jail here in Wautoma?

A I did.

Q And were just you and Deputy Spees present?

A That's right.

Q Now, you say that you had occasion to observe

123

him stripped, is that right?

A That's correct.

Q Who stripped him?

A He did himself.

Q He was asked to do that?

A He was.

Q By whom?

A By me.

Q Did you advise him of his rights?

MR. SUTTON: I object, your Honor. Under Schirmer versus California, he didn't have any rights.

MR. FRINZI: Pardon me?

THE COURT: He said he didn't haveany rights. Everybody has rights.

MR. SUTTON: Under Schirmer vesus California, he had no rights to refuse an eye - examination of his body.

MR. FRINZI: It's just a question, your Honor.

THE COURT: All right. Go ahead with your question.

MR. FRINZI: I'd like to make my record. If he wants to object, that's fine.

THE COURT: Go ahead.

MR. FRINZI: Did you advise Mr. Gein that he

124

didn't have to give any evidence against himself?

A I did.

Q What did you tell him?

A I told him that he was under arrest, and I advised him of his rights to an attorney, and if he didn't have the money to pay for an attorney, that the Court would furnish him one.

Q You told him that back in 1957?

A That's right.

Q Now, did you tell Mr. Gein that he didn't have to give any evidence against himself?

A I told him he had a right to an attorney.

Q I know, but did you tell him he didn't have to give any evidence against himself?

A I can't recall that I used those particular words.

Q Did you tell him that he had a right to remain silent - that he didn't have to say or do anything?

A I did.

Q What did you tell him?

A I wrote on that pad -- I'm sorry I can't produce it -- but I wrote on that pad, "I, Eddie Gein, knowing Dan Chase to be the County Officer," then I started questioning him.

125

Q You wrote that down but you didn't file it with the Sheriff?

A I don't know where it is.

Q I see. You don't know what you did with it? You put down there, "I Eddie Gein, knowing Dan Chase," is that all you put?

A "Knowing Dan Chase to be the Law Enforcement Officer for Waushara County."

Q That's what you told him?

A That's right.

Q Or put down on a paper?

A That's right.

Q Did you tell Mr. Gein that he didn't have to take his clothes off?

A No, I did not.

Q But you said you observed what appeared to be a spot of blood on his arm?

A I did.

Q Did you do anything about that spot that you saw?

A I didn't do anything about it, no.

Q Did you remove that spot?

A I did not.

Q Do you know how that spot got there?

A No, I do not.

126

Q   You don't know whether he bumped his arm
against the wall?

A   No.

Q   You don't know if --

MR. SUTTON: Object. All this is speculative.

THE COURT: Yes. He says he doesn't know
anything about it. That covers it.

MR. FRINZI: Q   Did you take a picture of the
condition of his arm with that spot?

A   No, I did not.

Q   Did you make a written report to any of your
superiors concerning your observation?

A   No, I did not.

Q   Did you make any kind of a report concerning
this observation about the spot of blood?

A   No, I did not.

Q   Now, did you make any kind of a written
report concerning your role in this Gein matter?

A   (Long pause.)

Q   Do you understand the question? I'll repeat
it:

        Did you at anytime, Mr. Chase, make a
written report concerning what you did in this
Gein matter from the 16th to the 17th, or 18th of
November, 1957?

                                    127

A   The only written report that I have is what
I wrote on the pad when I asked Eddie Gein to tell
me where he was from the time he got up until the
present time.

Q   What did you do with that written report?

A   I have it.

Q   Where is it?

A   In my possession.

Q   Can I see it?

A   You can.

Q   All right.

MR. SUTTON: Object. It's my understanding
that statements have been suppressed.

MR. FRINZI: We're not talking about statements.
I have a right to see what he did here.

MR. SUTTON: I'll withdraw my objection.

THE COURT: All right. Is this something you
wrote?

THE WITNESS: I wrote it.

MR. FRINZI: I'll ask him couple more questions.

THE COURT: I was just going to say: have you
seen it, Mr. Sutton?

MR. SUTTON: I don't know what he's referring to.

THE COURT: Will you produce it, Mr. Chase,
and let Mr. Sutton see it, and then let Mr. Frinzi
see it. Do you have it on you?

                                              128

THE WITNESS: No.

MR. FRINZI: What did you do with it?

THE WITNESS: A It's in my possession.

MR. FRINZI: You never filed that with the Sheriff's office or with your superiors, or any-thing?

THE WITNESS: A I never filed it with them.

Q You never made any other report except the one you claim you got?

A No, sir.

Q Could you, Mr. Chase, make this report available to the Court?

A I could.

MR. FRINZI: He's going to be here. He's the bailiff.

THE COURT: He can't go anywhere. He's got to be with us.

MR. FRINZI: That's all for now. We'll excuse him, and then --

MR. SUTTON: Where is the report right now?

THE WITNESS: It's locked in my -- in the jeep downstairs.

MR. SUTTON: I'd like to dispose of the matter if possible, now. We can take a recess.

129

THE WITNESS: I can run and get it.

THE COURT: Don't run.

(Short recess taken.)

MR. FRINZI: Now, Mr. Chase, you have had an opportunity to read over your notes of November 16, 1957, right?

A That's right.

Q And, in reading over those notes, you had an opportunity to refresh your memory, right?

A Some.

Q Now, will you tell the Court whether or not anywhere in those notes do you have a notation that you observed a spot of blood on the arm of Edward Gein?

A No, there is none.

MR. FRINZI: Okay. That's all.

THE COURT: Thank you, Mr. Chase.

Mr. Sutton?

MR. SUTTON: Would you like to have the notes marked and put in evidence?

MR. FRINZI: No. If I wanted them marked I would have done it. You try your case, I'll try mine.

REDIRECT EXAMINATION

BY

MR. SUTTON:

130

Q   Mr. Chase, you're familiar with the Worden Hardware Store in Plainfield?

A   I am.

Q   Were you familiar with it on November 16, 1957?

A   I was.

Q   In what county is that store?

A   Plainfield.

Q   What county?

A   Waushara County.

Q   And are you familiar with -- you testified your familiar with the Gein residence?

A   I am.

Q   What county is the Gein farm in?

A   Waushara County.

MR. SUTTON: That's all.

MR. FRINZI: No further questions.

MR. SUTTON: Mr. Goult, please.

                    RAYMOND A. GOULT

called as a witness herein, having been first duly sworn, was examined and testified as follows:

                    DIRECT EXAMINATION

                    BY

                    MR. SUTTON:

Q   What is your name, sir?

                                                        131

232

A   Raymond A. Goult.

Q   And your occupation?

A   Funeral Director.

Q   And where is your business located?

A   In Plainfield, Wisconsin.

Q   And how long has it been located there?

A   Oh, since 1900.

Q   How long have you operated the funeral home?

A   Since 1944.

Q   And were you so operating it on November 16, 1957?

A   Yes.

Q   Now, on the early morning of November 17, 1957, did you have occasion to go to the Gein farm in Waushara county?

A   Well, I think I was there in the early morning.

Q   And for what purpose did you go to the Gein residence?

MR. FRINZI: Object.   That calls for a conclusion.

THE COURT: He may answer.

THE WITNESS: I assumed that I was going to pick up the body of Bernice Worden.

MR. SUTTON: Q   Approximately what time did you get there, if you recall?

132

A   Well, I was called about 10:00 o'clock
in the evening on a Saturday night.

Q   Of the 16th of November?

A   Yes.

Q   What time did you get to the farm, approximately?

A   About 10:00 - a little after.

Q   How long were you on those premises?

A   Until 4:30 - 5:00 o'clock.

Q   What if anything did you do with the body
that was on those premises?

A   I brought it to Plainfield.

Q   And where did you take it in Plainfield?

A   To the funeral home.

Q   About what time did you take it --

A   About 4:00 o'clock.

THE COURT: Is this A.M.?

THE WITNESS: This is Sunday morning, yes.

MR. SUTTON: Q The 17th of November?

A   Yes.

Q   Now, did you have occasion to be present
at a post-mortem examination by Doctor Eigenberger?

A   I did.

Q   Who all was present at that time, to your
recollection?

A   Well, his wife.

Q Mrs. Eigenberger?

A Mrs. Eigenberger. And there was a man assigned by the Crime Lab, or someone, to stay with the body with me, and he was there until -- or somebody replacing him -- all during the next day.

Q Did you have occasion to see Mrs. Worden's head that morning?

A I did.

Q And where did you see that?

A Well, it was brought around 8:00 o'clock, I'd say.

Q Who brought it?

A Dan Chase.

Q Did he turn it over to you?

A That's right.

Q Did you know Mrs. Bernice Worden before that day?

A I did.

Q And at this time I show you what are in evidence as State's Exhibits 9, 10, and 11, and ask you if you will look at those and tell the Court what they are?

A They are pictures.

Q Of what?

A Well, of a head lying on something.

134

Q Do you recognize that head?

A Well, if this is the same head that was brought that morning --

MR. FRINZI: Hold it.

MR. SUTTON: Do you recognize the picture in the photograph?

MR. FRINZI: That was not responsive.

THE COURT: It will be stricken. Do you recognize the picture of the head?

THE WITNESS: A Yes. That's Mrs. Worden.

MR. SUTTON: Q Now, after the examination in your funeral home, what occurred? Did you go anywhere else that day?

A Yes. We came to Wautoma.

Q And where in Wautoma did you come?

A Doctor Darby's office.

Q And what occurred at Doctor Darby's office?

A Further examination of the head.

MR. SUTTON: All right. Your witness.

CROSS EXAMINATION

BY

MR. FRINZI:

Q Now, Mr. Goult, do you know of your own knowledge whether X-Rays of the head that was brought to your funeral home -- whether that head

135

was X-Rayed?

A I do. It was.

Q Were you present when it was X-Rayed?

A Yes.

Q Where were these X-Rays taken?

A In Doctor Darby's office.

Q Who was present?

A Doctor Darby.

Q Who else?

A The man from the Crime Lab.

Q Were you there?

A Yes, sir.

Q Now, were the X-Rays taken before or after the bullet had been removed from the head?

A Before.

Q Before the bullet had been removed?

A Yes.

Q Now, were you present at the time the cause of death of this body was determined? Were you present?

I'll withdraw the question and take it back this way:

Were you present when Doctor Eigenberger made a post-mortem examination of the body that was in your funeral home?

136

A   All the time, yes, sir.

Q   And, that was conducted at your funeral
home?

A   Yes. That's right.

Q   Now, at that time, do you know whether or
not the cause of death of this body was determined
before or after the X-Rays had been taken?

A   I think after.

Q   I see. You think. You're not sure?

A   I'm sure. The final decision was --

Q   The final decision?

A   -- as to the cause of death was made.

Q   Was made after the X-Rays?

A   Yes.

Q   Now, you say that this Doctor's name was
Darvy?

THE COURT: Darby.

MR. FRINZI: How do you spell that?

THE WITNESS: A D-a-r-b-y.

MR. FRINZI: Q Is he still living here in
Wautoma?

A   Yes.

Q   Where is his office?

A   Well, it's in the same office next to the
lumber yard there.

137

Q   Is that on North St. Marie Street?

A   Whatever it is.

MR. FRINZI: That's all, sir.

MR. SUTTON: You may step down.

MR. FRINZI: He's a business man. He can be excused. I don't want to hold him up.

MR. SUTTON: Mrs. Eigenberger, please.

CORDILIA EIGENBERGER

called as a witness herein, having been first duly sworn, was examined and testified as follows:

DIRECT EXAMINATION

BY

MR. SUTTON:

Q   What is your name?

A   Cordilia Eigenberger.

Q   And your address?

A   1115 Greendale Road, Sheboygan.

Q   Is that Miss or Mrs. Eigenberger?

A   Mrs.

Q   What was your husbands name?

A   Doctor Friedy Eigenberger.

Q   Was he a physician?

A   Yes, sir.

Q   And, he passed away, is that correct?

A   Yes, sir. 1961.

138

Q   Now, I direct your attention to November 16, 1957, where did you live at that time?

A   At the same address, sir.

Q   On November 16, or 17, 1957, did you have occasion to come to Waushara County, Wisconsin?

A   Yes, sir, on November 17.

Q   Who came with you, if anyone?

A   My husband, Doctor Eigenberger, and Sheriff Harold Kroll, and Robert Frewert.

Q   What mode of transportation did you use?

A   It was the Sheriff's car, sir.

Q   Approximately what time did you get to Waushara County?

A   I'd say it must have been about 10:00.

Q   And where did you go when you came to Waushara County? What Community?

A   We went to Plainfield.

Q   And, where in Plainfield did you go?

A   I don't remember where we went first, but we did go to various places, and among them to the funeral home, and to the hardware store.

Q   Now, at the funeral home, what if anything occurred?

A   At the funeral home the Doctor performed a post-mortem examination.

139

Q Were you present when that post-mortem was
conducted?

A Yes, sir, I was.

Q Who else was present to your recollection?

A The funeral director, and there were many
other people, but -- men from the State Crime Lab --
the people were going in and out there.

Q Now, did you perform any service while your
husband was conducting the post-mortem?

A Yes, sir, I did.

Q Would you describe that?

A I took some notes while he was doing the
work. He dictated some notes he was to have me
keep.

Q Now, before that time had you ever had
occasion to take notes under similar circumstances?

A Many times, sir.

Q What kind of training did you have for that
purpose?

A I was the secretary and office manager in
a large medical clinic in Sheboygan.

Q Now, after the post-mortem was conducted
at the funeral home, did you have occasion to be in
the Coroners office in Wautoma?

A Yes, sir.

140

Q   And, would you describe what transpired there?

A   We had taken the head there for X-Rays, and to determine to try to find the bullet.

Q   Did you take notes there from your husband's dictation?

A   Yes, sir.

Q   Do you have those notes with you?

A   Yes, I do.

MR. SUTTON: Would you please mark this envelope State's Exhibit 12 for Identification?

> (Whereupon, said documents were
> marked Plaintiff's Exhibit
> No. 12 for Identification.)

Let the record reflect that the witness has given me an envelope containing twenty pages.

MR. FRINZI: The record don't have to reflect that if he's got an Exhibit.

MR. SUTTON: I'm simply doing it so I don't have to mark from 12 to 32.

THE COURT: Exhibit 12 is the envelope which, as I understand it, contains twenty sheets of paper?

MR. SUTTON: Are those notes in shorthand, Mrs. Eigenberger?

THE WITNESS: No, sir.

141

MR. SUTTON: Mr. Frinzi has suggested that each piece of paper be identified and marked, and we can mark it 12A, B --

THE COURT: The Reporter will mark it A, B and so forth.

MR. FRINZI: Before we do that, let's find out from the witness if the're in chronological order.

MR. SUTTON: I'll allow Mr. Frinzi to cross examine.

MR. FRINZI: I'm saving time. This has nothing to do with cross examination'.

THE COURT: That seems sensible to the Court. Let the witness examine them and see if the're in chronological order, and if they aren't, please arrange them that way in the order as you took them.

Are they in order?

THE WITNESS: Yes, sir.

THE COURT: All right, hand them to Mr. Brillowski and he will mark them A, B, C, and so forth.

(Whereupon, said documents were marked Plaintiff's Exhibits Nos. 12A through 12T for Identification.)

142

What has been marked State's Exhibits
12A through 12T, those notes were made contemporaneous
with your husband on November 17, 1957?

A   Yes.

Q   Where have those notes been in the interim
period from 1957 to today?

A   They have been in a sealed envelope in my
home.

MR. SUTTON: At this time I'd like to offer
into evidence what has been marked State's Exhibits
12A to 12T.

THE COURT: Any question about them?

MR. FRINZI: No.

THE COURT: They will be received.

> (Whereupon, Plaintiff's Exhibits
> Nos. 12A through 12T for
> Identification were received
> in evidence.)

MR. SUTTON: I'd like to have you mark this
document State's Exhibit No. 13 for Identification
and number each page alphabetically.

> (Whereupon, said documents were
> marked Plaintiff's Exhibits
> Nos. 13A through 13J and 14
> for Identification.)

143

I would offer into evidence what have been marked State's Exhibits 13A through 13J for Identification as 13A through 13J in evidence, the autopsy protocol typed under and over the signature of Doctor Eigenberger, to which I understand the defense will stipulate.

MR. FRINZI: Yes, except I want to ask her not impeaching questions but few explanatory questions.

THE COURT: You want to do that before I receive it?

MR. FRINZI: No, you can receive it.

THE COURT: Just for the record, Exhibit 13 is received.

(Whereupon, Plaintiff's Exhibit Nos. 13A through 13J for Identification were received in evidence.)

MR. SUTTON: And, I would offer into evidence what has been marked State's Exhibit 14, the death certificate, certified by the Deputy Register of this County.

THE COURT: I assume there is no question?

MR. FRINZI: No question.

THE COURT: Exhibit 14 is received.

144

(Whereupon, Plaintiff's Exhibit

No. 14 for Identification was

received in evidence.)

MR. SUTTON: I have a few explanatory questions also.

Mrs. Eigenberger, your husband was a graduate of a duly accredited medical school, was he not.

THE WITNESS: A Yes.

Q And, he had special training in Pathology, had he not.

A Yes.

Q And, at the time of this examination he was licensed to practice medicine and his credentials were on file in Wisconsin, were they not.

A Yes.

MR. SUTTON: Your witness.

CROSS EXAMINATION

BY

MR. FRINZI:

Q Was his license on file with the Clerk of Courts in the city of Sheboygan?

A It would have been the correct procedure.

Q With the proper authorities?

A With the proper authorities, yes.

145

Q   Now, Mrs. Eigenberger, you took the notes which are reflected in Exhibit 12, right? And from those notes this report was prepared? Did you prepare this report?

A   No, sir.

Q   But, this report was prepared from these notes that you took?

A   These are pertinent notes, and he did this.

Q   And incorporated by your husband into Exhibit 13?

A·   Yes, sir.

Q   The information he gave you that you took down, the material in Exhibit 12 is reflected in Exhibit 13?

A   Yes.

Q   Do you recognize this as your husband's signature?

A   Yes.

Q   There is only one more question, and that is this: This Exhibit 13, when your husband refers to left and right, how do we determine left and right? Left and right on the body of the individual that the examination was conducted of, or in respect to the way the Doctor viewed the body? Do you know?

146

THE COURT: Maybe it would be helpful to show in the report what your referring to.

MR. FRINZI: All right. While we're finding the copy, I'll ask her another question:

Now, were you present when the X-Rays were taken of the head?

A I was in the office.

Q I see. Do you know where those X-Rays are?

A No, sir.

Q Do you know to whom they were given?

A No.

Q Did your husband take the X-Rays?

A No, sir.

Q But they were taken at a Doctors office here in Wautoma?

A Yes, sir.

Q And, did your husband take them or did the other Doctor take them?

A My husband did not.

Q He didn't take them?

A No.

MR. FRINZI: Is it all right if we use my marked copy rather than the original?

MR. SUTTON: I'd rather you use the original.

MR. FRINZI: All right.

147

Now, Mrs. Eigenberger, on page 7 of Exhibit 13, at this point here where it reads, "the one on the left side appeared as a round hole." Now, when your husband is referring to the left side, how does he arrive at that direction, from the way he views the body or the way the body is, or don't you know?

A I wouldn't know, sir.

MR. FRINZI: All right, that's all.

Did your husband receive, to your knowledge any copies of the X-Rays that were taken of the head?

THE WITNESS: A I wouldn't know, sir.

MR. FRINZI: Did you see the X-Rays?

THE WITNESS: A Not I, sir.

MR. FRINZI: That's all.

At this time I'd like to make a demand --

THE COURT: Is that all, Mr. Sutton?

MR. FRINZI: This lady comes from Sheboygan. I have no objection if she wants to be excused. I don't have any intentions of calling her back. I don't know about Mr. Sutton.

MR. SUTTON: Not to my knowledge.

MR. FRINZI: If she wants to go back home she can go back to Sheboygan.

148

THE COURT: You can go back to Sheboygan, Mrs. Eigenberger. It's a nice town. I was there last week.

THE WITNESS: Thank you, sir.

MR. FRINZI: Now, I want to make a demand on the Prosecutor to turn over to the defense for examination by a Pathologist the X-Rays. If the State has those X-Rays, we'd like to make a demand so we can have our experts view those X-Rays, your Honor.

THE COURT: Do we have the X-Rays, do you know?

MR. SUTTON: Not to my knowledge, your Honor, and I'm not familiar with this type of procedure. A motion at this juncture in the trial, I don't consider --

MR. FRINZI: Well --

MR. SUTTON: Can I finish?

I don't consider them to be of any relevance to that particular part of the testimony.

I'll make an inquiry and determine what is available. I have no objection to him seeing them.

THE COURT: When you get an opportunity, will you check, I assume, with Doctor Darby, and if he has the X-Rays, let them be brought into Court.

MR. FRINZI: I think we can work that out

149

between Counsel.

THE COURT: Sure you can.

MR. FRINZI: Thank you, Mr. Sutton.

MR. SUTTON: At this juncture I'd like to ask for a recess. Things have proceeded far more rapidly than I anticipated.

THE COURT: Okay.

(Short recess taken.)

ALLAN WILIMOVSKY

recalled to the stand, having been previously duly sworn, on oath was further examined and testified as follows:

DIRECT EXAMINATION (cont'd.)

BY

MR. SUTTON:

Q What is your name?

A Allan Wilimovsky.

Q And you testified prior in this trial?

A I have.

Q You understand you're still under oath?

A Yes.

Q Now, what position do you hold at the State Crime Lab?

A I hold the position of Firearms Identification Specialist.

150

Q   And does this position occupy your full time?

A   It does.

Q   And, how long have you been engaged in this type of work?

A   Approximately nineteen and a half years.

Q   Would you please give a general description of your duties as a Firearms Identification Specialist?

A   Generally, these duties consist of receiving firearms, fired bullets, cartridge cases, ammunition, and related items, and the performance of examinations, and comparisons involving these items, and the rendering of reports covering the determinations made.

Q   Are these examinations conducted routinely by you in the course of your work in the Laboratory?

A   They are.

Q   And, what is the nature and extent of the training and the experience you have had to prepare you for the work you are now doing at the Lab?

A   As I stated, I have approximately nineteen and a half years of experience in the field of firearms identification.

In addition to my employment with the Wisconsin State Crime Laboratory, for a period of approximately twenty months I was assigned to the

151

United States Army Criminal Investigation Laboratory at Fort Gordon, Georgia. During this period of time I was assigned to the Firearms Identification Section.

I have had the opportunity to associate with and understudy several individuals who are recognized as being knowledgeable in the field of firearms identification.

I have further lectured to various law enforcement groups covering the general subject matter.

Q Have you ever acted as an instructor and lectured to law enforcement groups.relating to firearms identification?

A I have.

Q Have you ever testified as an expert witness in the field of firearms identification?

A I have.

Q On how many occasions?

A Approximately one hundred.

Q And, in November of 1957, were you also employed as a firearms identification specialist?

A I was.

Q Now, you testified, Mr. Wilimovsky, that you were present at the time that Doctor Eigenberger

152

recovered a bullet from the head of Mrs. Bernice
Worden. Do you have that bullet with you?

A It's on the table before me, yes.

MR. SUTTON: Mark this please.

(Whereupon, said object was
marked Plaintiff's Exhibit
No. 15 for Identification.)

I show you what has been marked --

MR. FRINZI: Hold it. May I see that a
minute?

(Mr. Sutton showing Exhibit
to Mr. Frinzi;)

There's nothing to see.

MR. SUTTON: I move that be stricken.

I show you State's Exhibit No. 15 for
Identification and ask you what that is?

THE WITNESS: A Exhibit 15 contains a .22
calibre fired bullet which was recovered from the
head by Doctor Eigenberger, and also contained
within Exhibit 15 is a glass vile in which I
placed the bullet at the time of its recovery. The
vile is banded, or was originally banded, with
adhesive tape which is marked by Doctor Eigenberger
and myself.

Q What if anything did you do with the bullet

153

after you did that?

A It remained in my possession until I
returned to Madison.

Q Now, I direct your attention to November 18,
1957, would you tell the Court whether or not you
had occasion to be on the Worden Store premises
on that day?

A I did.

Q Why did you go to the store?

A To conduct a cursory examination of the
store.

Q Who if anyone went with you?

A Mr. Halligan, a Mr. Beck, and I beleive
Deputy Arnold Fritz of Waushara County Sheriff's
Office.

Q Approximately what time on the 18th did
you get to the Worden Store?

A I don't recall this specific time. My
recollection is that it was late that day. I
don't know. To my recollection it was dark outside.

Q Did you enter the premises?

A I did.

Q And what if anything did you discover on
the premises? What observations did you make, first
of all?

154

A The observations which I made were of a general nature, and in addition I specifically was looking for any .22 calibre firearms that may have been on the premises.

Q And, did you discover any .22 calibre firearms on the premises?

A I did.

Q And where did you discover such a weapon?

A In a rifle rack behind the counter in the hardware store.

Q And, would you describe what if anything you did at that time with that rifle?

A I operated the action of the three rifles which I observed, and one of the three, as a result of operating the action, a fired cartridge case was ejected from the firearm.

Q What if anything did you do with that cartridge case?

A I immediately recovered it.

MR. SUTTON: Mark this State's Exhibit No. 16 for Identification.

> (Whereupon, said object was
> marked Plaintiff's Exhibit
> No. 16 for Identification.)

In what manner did you secure the cartridge

155

case?

A I placed the cartridge case in a small coin envelope, sealed the envelope with adhesive on the flap, and took possession of it.

Q And, where did you take that cartridge case ultimately?

A To Madison.

Q I show you what has been marked State's Exhibit No. 16 for Identification, and ask you what that is?

A State's Exhibit 16 contains a fired cartridge case, and a small coin envelope in which I placed the cartridge case after finding the cartridge case in a Remington .22 rim fire calibre, model 121 slide action rifle, bearing serial number 149099, at the Worden Hardware Store, on November 18, 1957.

Q Now, what did you do with the weapon itself?

A I don't recall if the weapon was left in the rifle rack or whether the weapon was removed from the store and placed in the Mobile Field Unit and locked.

Q Did you have occasion to secure the weapon on the 19th of November, 1957?

A I did.

156

Q What if anything did you do with the weapon at that time?

A On the 19th of November, 1957, I placed the weapon in a cardboard box, cradle fashion, I cradled the firearm in this cardboard box, it was placed in the trunk of the Sheriff's automobile, and was taken to Madison.

MR. SUTTON: Mark this State's Exhibit 17 for Identification.

(Whereupon, said object was marked Plaintiff's Exhibit No. 17 for Identification.)

Now, I show you State's Exhibit No. 17 for Identification and ask you what that is?

A State's Exhibit No. 17 is a Remington .22 rim fire calibre slide rifle, model 121, bearing serial number 149099, which I recovered from the rifle rack at the Worden Hardware Store on the 19th of November, 1957.

Q Directing your attention to Exhibits 15, 16, and 17, did you subsequently make any examination involving those Exhibits?

A I did.

Q And, what was the purpose of those examinations?

157

A   The purpose of the examination was to establish, if possible, whether or not the fired cartridge case, which I had ejected from the rifle, Exhibit 17, had been fired in the rifle, and whether or not the fired bullet contained in Exhibit 15, which was recovered from the head, as to whether or not this particular bullet had been fired from the rifle, Exhibit 17.

Q   Now, directing your attention to Exhibit 17, I ask you what examinations you made involving it?

A   I made a visual inspection of the firearm to determine its mechanical operating condition. I test fired the firearm, recovering the test fired bullets and cartridge cases for subsequent comparison purposes.

In addition, prior to test firing the rifle, I pushed through the bore clean white dry gun patches.

Q   And, what did the examinations disclose?

A   Examination revealed that the firearm was in mechanical operating condition, and as a result of comparison microscope examinations involving the test fired bullets and cartridge cases which I fired from the rifle, Exhibit 17, and comparing those tests with the fired cartridge case contained in Exhibit 16, and the fired bullet contained in Exhibit 15, it is

158

my opinion that Exhibit 15 had been fired from the rifle, Exhibit 17, and the fired cartridge case contained in Exhibit 16 had been fired in the rifle, Exhibit 17.

Q And, your conclusion is that the bullet in Mrs. Worden's head came from that rifle?

A The bullet recovered from the head, yes.

MR. SUTTON: Your witness.

CROSS EXAMINATION

BY

MR. FRINZI:

Q Now, did you make any other -- did you make any examination with reference to Exhibit 17 with reference to fingerprints?

A I did not personally accomplish this examination.

Q Pardon?

A I did not personally do so.

Q You didn't?

A I did not.

Q Do you know if anyone else did?

A I do.

Q Do you know who did it?

A Yes.

Q Who did?

A Mr. Jan Beck.   159

Q And, when was that examination conducted?

MR. SUTTON: Object. Beyond the scope of the examination.

THE COURT: If he knows.

THE WITNESS: A On the morning of the 19th of November, 1957.

MR. FRINZI: Q Now, where was this done?

A Worden Hardware Store in Plainfield.

Q Calling your attention to Exhibit 17, do you know whether or not that Exhibit has any safety device with reference to the trigger.

A It does.

Q Could you point that out to the Court?

A The rifle, Exhibit 17, has a cross bolt type safety which is located at the rear of the trigger guard.

Q You don't know what the condition of that safety device was on either November 15, 16, 17, or 18, or prior to your coming into contact with the Exhibit?

A No, I do not.

Q Now, I'd like to ask you to open up Exhibit 16, that is the bullet, and open up Exhibit No. 15. Can you open them up?

A Tear it, or is there a pair of scissors?

160

MR. FRINZI: I don't know. Judge?

THE COURT: Anyway you want to.

MR. FRINZI: We'll proceed and let that alone for a while.

Would you tell the Court whether or not you recall whether the safety device on Exhibit 17 was on or off at the time that you first came in contact with Exhibit 17? If you know.

A I don't recall.

Q At the time that you came in contact with Exhibit 17, when did you first test Exhibit 17?

A Referring to test firing the rifle?

Q Yes. When?

A Afternoon of the 19th of November.

Q Where was that done?

A Madison, Wisconsin, at the Crime Lab.

Q Do you recall at that time whether the Exhibit was in the condition as when you got it - when you received it?

A It remained under my control all this time.

Q Could you tell us, prior to your receiving it, what was the condition of the safety device at that time if you recall?

A I don't recall.

Q You don't recall?

161

Now, at that time, that is when you first recovered Exhibit 17, did you test the safety device to see whether it was working at that time or not?

A   I did.

Q   So, you have no knowledge as to whether, on the 16th, 17th, or 18th of November, as to what the condition of the safety device was on those days?

A   I do not.

Q   Whether it worked or not, you don't know?

A   I don't know.

Q   Now, as I understand your testimony, you said you recovered Exhibit 19 -- Exhibit 17 on the 19th day of November, 1957, is that correct?

A   Yes.

Q   When was the first time that you had seen Exhibit 17?

A   On the 18th of November.

Q   And, you saw this at the Worden Hardware Store, is that correct?

A   Yes.

Q   Now, do you know of your own knowledge whether or not Exhibit 17 was at the Hardware Store on the 16th or 17th day of November 1957?

A   I do not know.

Q   Now, who was present on the 18th day of

162

November, 1957, when you first saw Exhibit 17?

A Mr. Jan Beck, Mr. James Halligan, and if my memory serves me correctly, Deputy Sheriff Arnold Fritz of Waushara County.

Q Now, do you know if any of these men handled Exhibit 17 on that day? If you know.

A I do not know.

Q Did you touch Exhibit 17 on that day?

A On the 18th?

Q On the 18th.

A Yes.

Q I'm talking about Exhibit 17 on the 18th.

A Yes, I did.

Q You don't know who, if anyone, handled that Exhibit prior to the 18th of November, 1957?

A I do not.

Q You don't know whether that Exhibit was in the store all during that period of time from the 16th to the 18th?

A I do not.

Q Now, could you tell me what type of a bullet that is embraced in Exhibits 15 and 16?

A One is the cartridge, and one is the bullet.

Q What type of bullet is it?

A The fired cartridge case contained in

163

Exhibit 16 is a Remington manufactured .22 rim fired calibre cartridge case.

The fired bullet contained in Exhibit 15 is a .22 calibre plain lead type fired bullet consistent with Remington manufacture.

Q Now, are there different types of .22 bullets?

A Yes.

Q And, how many types are there?

A There is the .22 "BB" cap, the .22 "CB" cap, the .22 short, the .22 long, and the .22 long rifle, and the .22 rim fire magnum.

Q All of these .22 bullets that you are talking about, can they be used in Exhibit No. 17?

A All with the exception of the .22 rim fire magnum.

Q All but what?

A With the exception of a .22 rim fire magnum which is a longer cartridge than the others.

Q Are these .22 bullets that you testified to, are they of different sizes, or diameters?

A The diameters are quite consistent. The lengths will vary, and the widths will vary.

Q When you say the diameters are quite consistent, could you tell the Court whether or not the diameters vary on a millimeter basis.

164

A   Not on a millimeter basis.

Q   On what basis do they vary?

A   In terms of ten thousandths of an inch.

Q   But they do vary?

A   It's possible, yes.

Q   Now, what kind of .22 bullet is contained in Exhibit 15 and 16?

A   .22 rim fire calibre.

Q   Hold it. Not so fast.

A   .22 rim fire calibre of the plain lead type.

Q   Yes.

A   And it's consistent with the Remington manufacture.

Q   It's what?

A   It's consistent with Remington manufacture.

Q   What does that mean?

A   The manufacturer of the bullet. Remington.

Q   I see. When you say "consisting" --

A   Consistent.

Q   -- that means that the manufacturer is Remington?

A   Yes.

    Further, the bullet, by its base cavity, is further consistent with a .22 rim fire calibre short bullet.

165

Q Now, you testified, I beleive, that a .22 rim fire magnum would not fit into this type of a rifle as is reflected in Exhibit No. 17, is that correct?

A Yes.

Q Now, you testified that there were other types of .22's, is that correct?

.22 "BB", what is the diameter of a .22 "BB", if you know?

A It's approximately .225 inches in diameter.

Q Is that diameter larger or smaller than the diameter of a .22 rim fire magnum?

A It's approximately the same, a plus or minus several ten thousandths of an inch.

Q When you say a .22 rim fire magnum would not operate or fit in Exhibit 17, what do you mean by that?

A The overall length of the .22 rim fire magnum cartridge exceeds the length of the chamber of the barrel in the rifle, Exhibit 17. It's too long to be inserted. The .22 rim fire magnum is too long to be inserted into the chamber of the rifle, Exhibit 17.

Q Is that the only reason why a .22 rim fire magnum can't fit into Exhibit 17, because of the

166

267

length and not diameter or width?

A Yes.

Q What is the difference between a .22 rim fire long, and a .22 rim fire short?

A The overall cartridge length.

Q The cartridge length?

A Length.

Q What is the difference in measurement?

A I don't have that information at my finger tips.

Q Pardon me?

A I don't have that information.

Q You don't know?

A The information is available to me.

Q But you don't know it right now?

A No, I don't.

Q You don't have knowledge right now of the difference?

A The .22 long --

Q We know the information is there but do you know?

MR. SUTTON: Object as arguementative.

THE COURT: Wait wait. One at a time.

MR. FRINZI: Q Do you know what the difference between a .22 rim fire long or short is?

167

268

THE WITNESS: A Yes.

Q What is the difference?

A One is larger than the other. Overall length.

Q Now, looking at Exhibit No. 17, what is the ideal type of ammunition for Exhibit No. 17?

A It's my belief this would be dependent upon the individuals preference.

Q Will you explain that to the Court?

A Well, the possessor of a firearm would be the individual to determine whether or not he would elect to shoot in a rifle, such as Exihibit 17, the .22 short, long, or long rifle. The rifle is chambered for all three cartridges.

Q Are there rifles that are chambered only for short, or only for long?

A I'm aware of --

Q I'm talking about .22's now.

A I'm aware of rifles that are chambered solely for the .22 short, and solely for the .22 long rifle. Offhand I do not know of any rifle -- or at least commercially available at this time -- that is chambered for the .22 long only.

Q You say this was a .22 rim fire calibre?

A Yes.

168

Q   Now, could you compare that type -- that bullet and cartridge referred to in Exhibits 15 and 16 -- could you compare that with a .22 rim fire long, and a .22 rim fire short?

A   Well, the fired cartridge case contained in Exhibit 16 is a .22 rim fire short. The bullet contained in Exhibit 15 is consistent with a .22 rim fire short bullet.

Q   Now, Exhibit 17, could you tell what performance an individual would get if he used a .22 rim fire long in Exhibit 17 - if he used that type of a bullet?

A   Performance in what sense?

Q   As far as results.

A   The firearm will handle interchangeably with the short, long, and long rifle. The results would vary with respect to these cartridges along the lines of velocity and possible impact energy. They may vary.

Q   What does slide action mean?

A   Slide or pump action is the type of mechanical movement which is required to function a specific type of firearm.

Q   Could you demonstrate that to the Court?

A   Yes.

Q   Would you?

169

(Witness demonstrating.)

Q Now, if someone were trying that Exhibit out - 17 - to see if a bullet would fit in there, could you demonstrate that to us? How would he go about that?

A There are two ways that this can be accomplished, one of which would be to insert the cartridge thru the opening on the right-hand side of the receiver - physically inserting the cartridge into the chamber of the rifle.

The other method would be to remove the inner magazine tube or withdraw it to a point which exposes the loading port of the tubular magazine. The cartridge would be then inserted, base first, permitting it to be dropped into the tube. The inner tube would then be depressed into its locked position.

In order to bring the cartridge from the magazine into the chamber would require the functioning of the firearm to bring the cartridge into the chamber ready for firing.

Q Will you explain that last part where you slid the -- loading the magazine tube -- when you snapped the chamber back into place?

A I don't know if I quite understand?

Q You want to pull that magazine part out

170

again?

    A All right.

    Q Now, would you explain that part again? You claim you put the cartridge into that opening?

    A Yes.

    Q Now, continue from there.

    A The cartridge is placed in the loading port of the magazine tube.

    Q Right.

    A The inner magazine tube is then placed in its locked position. Contained within this inner tube, the inner magazine tube, is a spring and plunger which is termed the magazine follower. As a result of placing the magazine tube in its locked position, it forces the cartridge toward the butt end of the rifle, or that portion which is connected with the receiver.

    In order to get the cartridge, or to move the cartridge from the magazine tube into the chamber, requires the mechanical functioning of the rifle, pulling the slide back, which would permit the cartridge to enter the receiver portion of the rifle, and then forward motion of the slide action would then lift the cartridge and insert it in the chamber ready for firing.

171

THE COURT: We'll take a short recess.

(Short recess taken.)

MR. FRINZI: Now, Mr. Wilimovsky, you testified that you discovered some firearms in the home of Ed Gein, is that correct?

A Yes.

Q And, you also testified that Exhibit 17 was turned over to you on the 18th of November, or was it the 19th of November of 1957?

A I first saw Exhibit 17 on the 18th of November, and on the 19th of November I took possession of the firearm.

Q Could you tell the Court what the normal use that Exhibit 17 is put to?

A Generally a firearm of this type is intended for target shooting or small game hunting.

Q Now, comparing Exhibit 17 with the firearms that you found, or saw in the Gein residence, what would you say was the use of -- I believe you said you recovered a revolver in the Gein home?

A Yes.

Q What would be the use of that type of firearm that you recovered in the Gein residence?

A Generally a revolver of that type would be used for target shooting.

172

Q Would you tell us whether or not the action
of that firearm is greater than the action of
Exhibit 17?

A I don't quite understand what you mean,
Mr. Frinzi.

Q The power rather of Exhibit -- of the
firearm you recovered from the Gein home. Is the
power greater or lesser than the power in Exhibit
17?

A Of the revolver now that I recovered from
the residence?

Q Is the power greater there than the power
in Exhibit 17?

A They were both of the same calibre, .22 rim
fire, therefore, the power would be essentially the
same.

Q As I understand it, that was a .32 that you
said you saw, not a .22?

A The .32 that I testified with respect to
was an auto-loading pistol, not a revolver.

Q Would you compare the firearm with the
power of Exhibit 17?

A The .32 automatic pistol cartridge is
greater -- the bullet -- referring specifically to
the bullet -- the bullet is greater in weight, it's
larger in diameter, and it has less velocity than 173

the .22.

Offhand I don't know what the relative comparison of the impact energies are of the .32 automatic pistol cartridge.

The .32 automatic pistol cartridge is used in firearms which have been used for military purposes, and for police purposes.

Q   Now, is the power of that firearm greater than the power of Exhibit 17? That's my question.

A   I don't quite understand what you mean with respect to power.

Q   Well, the deadening effect of a discharge of a bullet in the .32 as compared to the deadly effect of a discharge of a bullet in Exhibit 17.

A   It's my belief this would depend upon where the bullet strikes the object.

Q   In other words, it's your opinion, as an expert, that there is no difference in power between Exhibit 17 and the .32 calibre revolver that you recovered in the Gein home?

A   There are differences, yes.

Q   What are those differences?

A   As I mentioned, the weight and the diameter.

Q   Is there greater weight in Exhibit 17, or in the .32 revolver?

174

is a full metal jacket type projectile, has a weight of approximately 71 grains.

Q Is it greater than Exhibit 17?

A Yes.

Q You testified that you recovered in Exhibit 17, Exhibit 15 and 16, a .22 rim fire short, isn't that your testimony? The bullet, Exhibit 15 and 16, one is the bullet and one is the cartridge?

A Yes.

Q I believe you testified it was your opinion that it was a .22 rim fire short?

A I believe my testimony was that the bullet contained in Exhibit 15 is consistent with a .22 calibre plain lead type short bullet, and the cartridge case, which is of Remington manufacture, is of the .22 rim fire short type.

Q Right. Now, there is a difference between a short and a long you said also?

A Yes.

Q Now, what is the difference with reference to the deadly effects between the long and the short?

A If I interpret your question, my answer would be the same: that in my belief it would be dependant upon where the object was struck by the

175

bullet.

Q Would you say that there is no difference then between a long and a short?

A There are differences, yes.

Q What are the differences?

A The overall length of the cartridge, the --

Q Now, would you use a .22 rim fire short to go out and shoot a deer?

A This is prohibited by law.

Q Assuming the law -- assuming there was no such law, would you go out and shoot a deer with a .22 rim fire short?

MR. SUTTON: Object. It's totally immaterial and speculative.

MR. FRINZI: He holds himself out as an expert on firearms.

THE COURT: I don't see too much materiality. I assume, Mr. Frinzi, what your asking him is whether or not the .22 would kill a deer.

MR. FRINZI: That's right.

Would a .22 rim fire kill a deer?

THE WITNESS: A If the bullet was properly placed upon the target, it's my belief that it would.

Q Now, you testified that you found a mauser

176

277

or saw a mauser in the Gein residence, is that correct?

A Yes.

Q What kind of a mauser was that?

A A German mauser, model 1910, .32 automatic pistol calibre, automatic loading pistol.

Q Would you compare that firearm with Exhibit 17 as far as deadening effects?

A I believe I essentially covered that, but --

Q You haven't on this comparison between the mauser and this Exhibit 17.

A Yes, we were discussing the .32 pistol.

THE COURT: The mauser is the .32 that he was talking about.

MR. FRINZI: I'm sorry. There was another firearm other than the .32 mauser.

THE WITNESS: Yes. There was a .32 calibre revolver that I made reference to.

MR. FRINZI: Q And then there was another one I believe you testified to.

A There were several others.

Q Do you know what the others were?

A I don't know the number that were represented, but they consisted of .22 calibre shoulder guns or rifles, and shotguns.

177

Q   Now, would you tell the Court, referring to Exhibit 17, the manner in which a bullet may be discharged? What ways could the bullet be discharged with reference to Exhibit 17?

A   The normal manner of discharging a cartridge in the rifle, Exhibit 17 would be, of course, to have the cartridge in the chamber, and then to pull the trigger.

Q   Any other ways in which a bullet may be discharged from the chamber other than by pulling the trigger?

A   With respect to Exhibit 17, when I conducted my examination involving it, I found it to be in mechanical operating condition with the safety features functioning.

Q   That's not my question. Is there any other ways other than by pulling the trigger for the bullet to be discharged from the chamber of Exhibit 17?

A   Yes, there would be.

Q   What are those other ways?

A   This one other way is a --

Q   Hold it. Is there more than one way other than by pulling a trigger for a bullet to discharge from the chamber? You said there was one other way. Are there other ways?

178

A I said the other way.

Q Will you tell us the other way?

A There would be the remote possiblity of a slam fire. And by using the term "slam fire" I refer to a cartridge being contained in the chamber of the rifle and then by rapidly and forcefully pushing the forearm forward causing the bolt to come forward and making contact with the cartridge, crushing the rim between the bolt face and the edge of the chamber.

Q Now, Mr. Wilimovsky, as a firearms expert, assuming that you wanted to kill someone --

MR. SUTTON: Object to this as speculative.

MR. FRINZI: I haven't finished the question. Give me the courtesy to finish the question anyway.

THE COURT: Let him finish the question.

MR. FRINZI: Q As a firearms expert, and assuming you wanted to kill someone, would you use a .22 short or a mauser if you had your choice of weapons?

MR. SUTTON: Object. It's immaterial and speculative.

MR. FRINZI: This goes too intent.

THE COURT: No. Sustained.

MR. FRINZI: I didn't hear the Court.

179

THE COURT: Sustained.

MR. FRINZI: My purpose here goes to the element of intent, your Honor.

THE COURT: It's too remote for that, I think.

MR. FRINZI: That's all.

MR. SUTTON: I have a few questions.

THE COURT: Just a minute.

MR. FRINZI: I'll ask one more question before I let him go.

Do you know who has this mauser?

THE WITNESS: A Yes.

Q Where is it?

A Locked in the gun room vault at the Crime Laboratory in Madison under my control.

Q And the .32 and the other firearms, do you know where they are? Are they in the Crime Lab?

A Yes.

Q You don't have them here in Wautoma with you?

A No, I do not.

MR. FRINZI: That's all.

REDIRECT EXAMINATION

BY

MR. SUTTON:

Q Mr. Wilimovsky, when you secured the weapon and transported it to Madison, would you describe how you held it?

180

A My first physical contact with the rifle,
Exhibit 17, which was on the night of November 18,
1957, the rifle was in the rifle rack at the Worden
Hardware Store, it was in a vertical position with
the butt down, the barrel was supported by a cut
out piece of wood, and I grasped the end of the
magazine tube, and simultaneously depressed the
action release button which is located on the under
side of the receiver.

I further pushed the magazine tube down
which caused the cartridge case that was chambered
in the firearm to be extracted and ejected.

The next contact - physical contact - that
I had with the rifle: the rifle was handled by the
end of the magazine tube and by the edge of the
trigger guard, the rifle was cradled in a cardboard
box, placed in the trunk of a vehicle, and transported
to Madison, and I was an occupant of that vehicle.

Q Did you handle this weapon in this manner
intentionally?

A I did.

Q For what purpose?

A For purposes of finger print identification.

MR. SUTTON: That's all.

MR. FRINZI: No questions.

181

THE COURT: The Court has one.

How would this particular rifle be normally loaded?

THE WITNESS: The normal loading procedure would be the withdrawal of the inner magazine tube and inserting the cartridges through the port in the magazine, and then re-inserting the inner tube and then working the action chamber.

THE COURT: Okay.

MR. SUTTON: At this time the State offers into evidence what have been marked Exhibits 15, 16 and 17.

MR. FRINZI: At this time I object on the grounds that the proper evidentiary escort has not been shown up to now. The testimony here is that -- we have had testimony that people went into the Worden Hardware Store on the 16th, and Mr. Wilimovsky said he saw Exhibit 17 on the 18th, and he didn't get it until the 19th, and there is nothing in the record, your Honor, to show under whose control the exhibit has been during the previous days.

THE COURT: So far as Exhibit 15 is concerned, the testimony was that the Doctor removed this from the head and delivered it to Mr. Wilimovsky, and he's

182

had it ever since. So, that takes care of 15,
doesn't it?

MR. FRINZI: Yes.

THE COURT: 16, as I recall the testimony, was
that he ejected it from the gun in the Worden
Hardware Store that day and he's had possession of
it everyday since, right?

MR. FRINZI: Yes, but they haven't shown,
your Honor, with reference to 16 and 17 -- maybe
15 I can see up to now they have shown the bullet
was taken from the head by the Doctor and given to
them -- but 16 and 17, there hasn't been a proper
evidentiary escort.

MR. SUTTON: May I be heard.

THE COURT: Sure.

MR. SUTTON: It's totally immaterial. All I
proved by that testimony was that that bullet and
cartridge come from that gun. It doesn't matter if
it was handled by all the citizens of Wautoma from
that day forward.

MR. FRINZI: There's no proof that that gun
was found there on the 16th.

MR. SUTTON: There's evidence here that that
gun was found there on the 18th, and that the bullet
came from that gun, and that the bullet was found

183

in the head of Mrs. Bernice Worden on the 17th, and that Mrs. Bernice Worden's head was found on Mr. Gein's premises. The whole point is that I'd have to argue the whole circumstantial evidence part of this case. There's been no challenge by cross examination related to the material evidence that comes from those two exhibits, which is that the bullet found in Mrs. Worden's head came from that gun.

THE COURT: Exhibits 15, 16 and 17 are received.

(Whereupon, Plaintiff's Exhibit Nos. 15, 16 and 17 for Identification were received in evidence.)

MR. SUTTON: Now, your Honor, at this juncture -- things have gone very rapidly today --

THE COURT: Yes. I must commend counsel on both sides.

MR. SUTTON: -- unexpectedly from my view point, and ask the Court indulgence to recess until morning.

I think I can fairly guarantee that we will close tomorrow, and probably by noon.

THE COURT: The Court will have no quarrel with you on that.

Shall we take a recess until 9:00 o'clock? Can we all get here by 9:00?

184

MR. FRINZI: I can.

MR. SUTTON: Yes.

THE COURT: All right, let's start at 9:00.

MR. FRINZI: You say you're going to finish by noon tomorrow?

MR. SUTTON: In all probabilities.

MR. FRINZI: Then that being the case, could we have until Tuesday to start the defense?

THE COURT: Well, that depends. I'll put it this way, Mr. Frinzi: I don't know whether you plan any defense in the first portion of this case, or whether you are simply talking about the defense on the insanity issue. Now, if there is defense on the first portion, I would assume we could go forward in the afternoon.

MR. FRINZI: I have a defense, but we'll have problems with some of the experts.

THE COURT: The Court will not mistreat you on it.

MR. FRINZI: It's a situation, your Honor, out of my control. I was led to believe that the State was going to take two or three days, and as a result I have -- I think we'll burn that bridge when we get to it.

THE COURT: If your not ready, you can be sure

185

the Court will look on the request for adjournment
with great indulgence.

(Witness temporarily excused.)

(Whereupon, the proceedings
in the foregoing cause were
continued to Friday, November
11, 1968, at 9:00 o'clock a.m.)

186

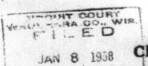
Form No. 5

State of Wisconsin

CENTRAL STATE HOSPITAL

PSYCHOLOGICAL DEPARTMENT

- 1 -

Name GEIN, Edward   Number 2753

December 4, 1957, by Mr. Ellsworth

The patient is a shy, 51-year-old, white male. He is a rather short person of wiry build and has short, greying hair and pale blue eyes. In the interviews and test situations, he was friendly and co-operated to the best of his ability. His speech was spontaneous, which, on occasions, became rambling in nature. He verbalized several physical complaints, such as double and blurred vision, dizziness, headaches, shooting pains in his neck, stomach trouble, and pressure like a tight band around his head. The patient talks of "forces" which were uncontrollable, that made him do the things he did over the past several years. He also gives the heart attacks suffered by his mother and his mother's death a peculiar twist: first, he blames himself for letting her into situations which caused the attacks; and second, he blames the people's actions at those times for bringing on the attacks. His reasoning here is not too realistic. There is also reference to visions, but it is difficult to obtain a clear explanation.

The patient's manner is calm with occasional jesting. At the present time, he is oriented as to place and person but has some difficulty in giving the date. His recent memory is good. His remote memory is also good except for facts surrounding some of the offenses. Here it seems that the patient has difficulty and becomes confused in separating and remembering data from that which has been presented to him in the past few months. His insight into his problems is rather superficial. He has shown poor judgment in dealing with his conflicts in the past.

TEST RESULTS

Wechsler Adult Intelligence Scale: Verbal I.Q., 106; Performance I.Q., 89; Full Scale I.Q., 99.

There is a large difference between the verbal and performance levels along with a large degree of variance among the subtests themselves, which would indicate emotional disturbance. However, with all of the visual motor subtest rather low, organicity should be considered. This possibility is weakened by the fact that he is able to complete the tasks providing he is allowed to exceed the time limit.

weeks in a year or Washington's birthday but getting more difficult items. Also, peculiar verbalizations are occasionally present along with poor planning and poor organizing ability.

His display of a fair amount of general information, good

288

Central State Hospital

State of Wisconsin
CENTRAL STATE HOSPITAL
PSYCHOLOGICAL DEPARTMENT

Name GEIN, Edward   - 2 -   Number 2753

<u>December 4, 1957</u>, by Mr. Ellsworth (continued)

vocabulary, and ability to reason abstractly points toward a higher intellectual potential, near the "bright normal" level, rather than the indicated "low average" at which he is functioning now.

In general, the impairments would indicate a strong emotional disturbance which would be psychotic in nature.

<u>Bender-Gestalt:</u> In view of possible organicity, this test was given to the patient. His reproductions here gave no indication of organic disturbance in the visual-motor area. This strengthens the hypothesis that the disturbance is functional rather than organic.

<u>Rorschach:</u> This test was started once but the subject's complaints of a severe headache discontinued the test until he felt better. On second testing, it was completed.

There are indications that subject is better than average intelligence, but here again is shown inefficient functioning. His productivity is not in keeping with his intellect and his thinking may be tangential and alogical at times. This is especially true when confronted with emotionally charged stimuli. His contact with reality is within range of adequacy but is probably kept there through an effort that takes much out of him. He is capable of recognizing the common events of existence but finds it difficult to accept and see the world in the same terms as others do, often discarding conforming views for less adequate ones.

The patient is a suggestible person who is colorless and emotionally dull. Yet, he is not too predictable and an undercurrent of aggressiveness that is present may be expressed by inappropriate reactions, followed by remorse and mild mannerness. He is also an immature and self-doubting person who is fearful in social contacts, letting others take the initiative.

In defense against the surfacing of conflicts and impulses, he uses withdrawal and repression. An inner tension is created by his strong effort to inhibit impulses. As shown by the history, his defenses weaken, at which time he deviates from the normal. At these times, he may have an exaggerated percept of himself and act accordingly.

The over-all picture is not that of a well person but of one with insufficient ego, immaturity, conflict concerning identification and possibly the presence of alogical thought processes.

<u>Figure Drawing:</u> The drawings give evidence of his being withdrawn and having a rather expansive fantasy life centering

December 4, 1957, by Mr. Ellsworth (continued)

around himself. He attempts to control drives and concern over bodily functions by intellectual inhibition. Sexual conflicts are present and appear to be centered around guilt feelings, identification, and voyeurism. There is evidence of some hostility, which he finds difficult to express.

T.A.T. and M.A.P.S.: In the more structured T.A.T., two of his stories centered around young girls and their boy friends, which is a peculiar twist for a man his age and background. Aggressive themes appear but are soon toned down or not carried out at all. It is also felt that feminine identification is present along with wishful thinking.

Going into the less structured M.A.P.S. where figures have to be placed on the background, the patient's initial comment upon seeing the figures was, "Oh, even ghosts." In setting up the situation, he showed poor organization and the figures he used were not in keeping with what has to date been found in the average person. The stories ended usually with a moral or with a warning about lack of temperance. One story displayed a rather morbid sense of humor. In some of the stories, peculiarities were present. They would suggest odd and possibly bizarre religious beliefs and project the blame for evil on alcohol or some other person. As found in other tests, there were conflicts concerning aggressiveness and identification. The M.A.P.S., in general, has a schizophrenic bend to it.

Rosenzweig P.F.: On this test we find an ego-defensive person who probably has various shortcomings and guilt feelings. He, therefore, attempts to project the blame mostly onto others or objects. On this test, he gave several very aggressive responses.

Blacky Pictures: Sexually, the subject is functioning at the pregenital stage of development. He is an orally dependent person who has guilt feelings concerning sexual activity. It is evident that he was quite close to his mother and probably felt rejected by the father.

M.M.P.I.: Records showing similar profiles as produced by the patient were those with complaints of headaches, pains in the back, and pains in the eyes. Any internal pains appeared to be precordial in location. The patient has expressed similar complaints on various occasions.

In spot checking some of his replies, he has very little faith or trust in people, difficulty concentrating, disturbed sleep, blank periods, and feelings of wanting to smash things at times. He also relates experiencing unusual events and visions, but gives an unclear

<u>December 4, 1957</u>; by Mr. Ellsworth (concluded)

explanation of what is meant.

<u>General Conclusions:</u> On superficial contact, this 51-year-old, white male appears fairly well intact; however, closer observation and test results indicate otherwise. His speech on occasions is rambling and his thinking is rather difficult to follow at times. No strong evidence of hallucinations and delusions were brought out in talking with him, since his explanations were rather vague. Concerning visions, his explanation referred to periods before he was born and had a rather bizarre trend to it. Physical complaints that were verbalized are mentioned previously. This shows some hysteroid components and tests gave some evidence of compulsion and phobic reactions.

The patient is a very suggestible person who appears emotionally dull. Beneath this lies aggressiveness that may be expressed by inappropriate reactions that are followed by remorse and mild mannerness. He is an immature person who withdraws and finds forming relationships with others difficult. He has rather rigid moral concepts which he expects others to follow. He is suspicious of others and tends to project blame for his own inadequacies onto others. His fantasy life is immature in nature, possibly pictures himself as a much more adequate and bigger man than he is.

Sexually, he is a conflicted individual and is functioning on an immature level. Guilt feelings are great and repression is put into use quite frequently in this area.

In general, it appears that this is basically a schizophrenic personality with several neurotic manifestations. At the present time, he is confused and has difficulty in looking at his situation realistically.

Robert E. Ellsworth
Psychologist

CENTRAL STATE HOSPITAL

SOCIAL SERVICE ~~CIRCUIT COURT~~ Number 2753
WAUSHARA CO., WIS.
FILED

Name GEIN, Edward   1

December 16, 1957 by Mr. Colwell   JAN 8 1978

SOCIAL HISTORY ... McCOMB, CLERK

Identifying Information: This 51 year old patient was admitted to Central State Hospital for 30 days observation under Statute 957.27(3) by order of Waushara County Circuit Court following a charge of Murder, First Degree.

Informants: The information in this report was obtained from the patient and other sources. The patient expressed a desire to be cooperative, indicating that this "was a job which must be done". The patient talks freely in a low voice, frequently with his head in his hands. He described incidents in his life with continuity, but on occasion would respond to a specific question by relating other aspects of his life history. He expressed appreciation for his treatment here and apparently viewed the Staff's professional approach as an acceptance of him personally that he has not experienced in his home community in many years. Patient appears to respond to suggestion, making questioning difficult. He professes confusion, partial loss of memory as well as trouble distinguishing between what he remembers and what he was told. He attributed difficulties in responding to not feeling well and to extensive interrogation both here and prior to admission here.

Present Offense: The patient's conversation indicated an acceptance of responsibility for the death of two women, but he denied prior motivation. He described an inability to recall significant details of the acts which he viewed as accidental. His recall of the grave robbing incidents was more complete.

Previous Offenses: The patient denied any previous criminal offenses or arrests.

Personal History: The patient's father, George Gein, died in 1940 at the age of 65 of a heart condition. He was born in Coon Valley, Wisconsin and was an orphan who had little opportunity for education. During the patient's early life, while in LaCrosse, the father worked in a tannery as a carpenter for the railroad and for the LaCrosse City Power Plant. When the patient was eight years old, the family moved to the farm in Plainfield which now belongs to the patient. The father was described as a heavy drinker who would become easily angered when inebriated. He "did not like to work" and on occasion the mother found jobs for him. The father drank less in later years and was a semi-invalid for sometime prior to his death.

<u>December 16, 1957</u> continued

The patient's mother, <u>Augusta nee Loehrke</u>, died in 1945 at the age of 64. She was described as the dominate parent who handled family decisions and, at times, managed the farm work. She was of German extraction and very thrifty, hard working and moralistic. The patient was closely identified with her, accepting her guidance and her demands. He described her courageousness even while bed ridden, stating that she never complained, but was able to "enjoy fun and make other people feel better".

The patient's brother, <u>Henry</u>, who was five years older, died in 1944. Both were treated equally well by the parents and adjusted well to each other except "for the usual arguments that brothers always have". The brother worked away from the farm much of the time and on one occasion was a foreman for a farmer who hired Jamaicans. "He was the only man in the area who could handle those guys". His death occurred when a marsh fire got out of control. The patient got one side of the fire under control and went to help his brother, but could not find him. He states that he got a search party and "when we returned, I went right to where he was". "Funny how that works". The patient assumes that the brother was either overcome by smoke or had a heart attack.

The patient describes his childhood as not happy due to the family's poor financial situation occasioned by the father's drinking and difficult job adjustments. The father was abusive when drunk and the mother had stated that she would have left the father except for the children. The family moved to the farm at Plainfield because the father wished to be independent. It would appear that the mother's moralistic preachings were not well accepted by the neighbors and the patient indicated that they were envious of the farm which was always neat and well cared for. It is probable that the family did not accept the habits of their neighbors and quite a point was made of the fact that Geins did not work on Sundays. He also stated that when "we came there the neighbors did not cooperate and tell us how to work the sandy soil".

The patient completed the eighth grade of school and got along well with his classmates, joining them in recreational and social activities when time could be spared from the farm work. After the completion of school he remained on the family farm. After more responsibility after the father's death. With the death of the brother, and the mother's invalidism, he was unable to operate the farm as efficiently. Following the mother's death he kept

December 16, 1957 continued

stock on the farm for a time, but began working out on a day to day basis with the neighbors. Later he sold the stock and the farm gradually deteriorated. He stated that he preferred to let it reseed itself to wood land. He had hoped to sell the farm, visit relatives throughout the country for a time and then settle down in some other part of the country. He felt that he was not accepted in the neighborhood and states "people would come to visit me, but I would soon find that they only came to borrow things or to ask for my help." He added that "we had always tried to be good neighbors but people took advantage of us". With the exception of a couple of families, he was not invited into other homes although "the women were kinder in this regard than the men folks."

For recreation the patient has skied most of his life and also practiced archery. He enjoyed watching basketball games and other sports events. He is interested in music and plays the violin, the accordian and the mouth organ. He enjoyed listening to music, preferring old time music to modern. He lost his interest in music after the mother's death. He frequently attended movies preferring adventure and western stories to love stories. He and the brother frequently attended dances but "we were too self-conscious to dance". He did, however, enjoy square dancing, for a time.

Sexual History: Patient's early sexual information was given by the mother who impressed upon him the need for sexual abstinence prior to marriage. He indicated that she was not as strong in her admonitions against masturbation. He obtained additional information in a more uncouth manner from his classmates. He views not marrying, in part, as a family trait saying that his brother did not marry, nor did two of his mother's brothers. The patient gave more thought to marriage after the death of the mother and felt he would have married if he could have found "the right girl". He rejected one girl after he learned that she could not get along with her mother and "I couldn't straighten her out on that. I almost fell in love with another girl, but found that she had had many affairs with other men. Morality is pretty low in Plainfield."

The patient also described the moral standards of his two victims. The first, "was a dirty talker, operated a tavern and people said that she was in some crooked business". He states that the second victim wooed her husband away from another girl and married him shortly after the other girl committed suicide.

December 16, 1957 continued

(He became tearful when describing his sorrow for the other girl.)
He went on to describe the husband's death as his just punishment
and then relates that his victim broke up another marriage. His
comments have a strong religious connotation.

The patient received religious training from his mother
whose strict teachings were unusual in the community but were not
viewed as excessive by the patient. He did not attend church
frequently because there was no Lutheran church in Plainfield.
After the mother's death he "turned away from God because he did
not feel it was right that his mother should have suffered so
much". Later he decided that "God knows best", and now feels that
the Bible gives him hope for the future.

He indicated that he would not have gotten into his present
difficulty if he had married, if the neighbors had treated him
better, or if he had been able to sell his farm and travel. He
stated that prior to the first grave robbing incident, he had
been reading adventure stories of head hunters and cannibals. He
related in detail one story of a man who had murdered a man,
acquired his yacht and was later captured and killed by head
hunters. He learned about shrunken heads, death masks, etc., from
other similar stories.

He admitted to feelings of excitement during the grave
robberies and describes periods when he felt he should return the
bodies. There were also feelings that the bodies should be
preserved and that he should care for them. When asked about the
sexual aspects of this activity he commented on the great
variations in age of the bodies. When it was pointed out that
he was interested only in the bodies of women, he stated that the
articles he read indicated that these heads were more valuable
because of their longer hair. Relative to the murders, he
recalled the sequence of events up to the act itself which
in the latter case he described as accidental, but had no recall
for his activity following the acts.

Kenneth Colwell

State of Wiscons.

CENTRAL STATE HOSPITAL

WAUPUN

December 19, 1957

he Honorable Herbert A. Bunde
th Circuit Court, Waushara County
Wisconsin Rapids, Wisconsin

ear Sir:

Re: Edward Gein

I am sending you a copy of the records in the case of Edward
Gein. Mr. Gein was seen by a board of doctors at Central State Hospital
on December 18, 1957. This board consisted of me, Dr. R. Warmington,
Chief of Medical Services; Dr. O. Larimore, Psychiatrist; Dr. O. Goetsch,
Physician; Dr. L. J. Ganser, Superintendent of the Diagnostic Center;
and Dr. H. J. Colgan, Clinical Director of the Winnebago State Hospital.
In addition to this group of doctors, Mr. Robert Ellsworth, Psychologist,
and Mr. Kenneth Colwell, Social Worker, also attended the meeting and
took part in the proceedings.

The staffing of Mr. Gein took several hours and consisted of
questions by the members, with the object of obtaining an opinion of
Mr. Gein's thinking and reactions. It was determined that Mr. Gein has
been suffering from a schizophrenic process for an undetermined number
of years and that this schizophrenic process is made apparent by what
is delusional thinking. He stated that his activities were the result
of some outside force acting upon him and that he had been chosen as
an instrument of God to carry out activities which were ordained to
happen. He also presented numerous somatic complaints for which there
is no physical basis and which must be considered in the nature of
somatic delusions. There have been at least several incidents of
olfactory, auditory and perhaps visual hallucinations in the last
twelve years.

The patient showed himself to be an extremely suggestible
individual who, without question, was inordinately emotionally attached
to his mother, and it was from her that his very strict moralistic
attitudes in regard to sex and drinking were obtained. It is not clear
what his motives were in violating the graves, since he claims at this
time that this activity was the result of an evil spirit influencing
him to engage in this activity. It seems probable that this activity
was the result of his desire to re-create the existence of his own mother.
After the death of his mother, he felt that he had a special power whereby he could raise the dead to life by an act of his will power; and when
he found that this was not successful, his emotional needs influenced
him to attempt the re-creation of his mother by using the parts of bodies
from other graves.

- 1 -

ADDRESS ALL CORRESPONDENCE CONCERNING PATIENTS TO THE SUPERINTENDENT

The Honorable Herbert A. Bunde   December 19, 1957
7th Circuit Court, Waushara County
Wisconsin Rapids, Wisconsin

Re: Edward Gein (concluded)

His opinion of Mrs. Worden was that she was a very loose and disreputable woman who deserved to die; and, although he now claims that her death was accidental, if such should be the case, his actions in bringing about her death were then unconsciously determined because of his judgment that she deserved this fate.

Although Mr. Gein might voice knowledge of the difference between right and wrong, his ability to make such judgment would be and is influenced by the existent mental illness. He would not be capable of fully realizing the consequence of any act because he would not be a free agent to determine either the nature or the consequence of acts which resulted from disturbed and abnormal thinking, which is part of his mental illness. Because of his extreme suggestibility and the nature of his mental illness, he is not completely or fully capable of acting in his own behalf in consultation with his attorney. Because of these findings, I must recommend his commitment to Central State Hospital as insane.

The 30-day observation period is up on the 22nd of December. I realize that no court action will be feasible because of the holidays. His confinement at Central State Hospital would certainly be acceptable to me; however, I would request your indulgence in sending me a statement indicating your desires in the matter.

Respectfully,

E. F. Schubert

E. F. Schubert, M. D.
Superintendent

EFS:mcl

Enclosures

297

State of Wisconsin

CENTRAL STATE HOSPITAL

Continued Notes

Consecutive Number 2753

Name GEIN, Edward   1

<u>November 25, 1957</u> by Dr. Warmington

    This patient was admitted on 11-23-57 for a 30 day observation period upon order of the Circuit Court of Waushara County after he had been arrested and charged with the crime of Murder, 1st Degree.

    Physical inspection disclosed a well developed, well nourished, middle-aged, white male that was ambulant and not in any apparent distress. A right inguinal hernia was noted and he asked about an abnormality in the left supraclavicular fossa that may be a lymph node overlying an arterial vessel with resultant pulsation transmission. Mentally he was found to be in contact with his surroundings, carried on a coherent conversation and verbalized without difficulty while speaking in a rather quiet, well modulated voice. He gave an adequate account of his past life and spoke some of the offense but no attempt was made to explore this in greater detail at this writing. He seemed to be fairly well at ease but mentioned being under strain and failing to sleep while under investigation prior to admission here. History indicates he has been closer to the mother than the father possibly since the father drank and was somewhat irritable on occasions. Mention was also made by him that he never married, has never had sexual relations and the impression was gained that he has been rather limited in his social contacts. At this time he also seems to recognize this as for example he thinks that it might have been better if he had been drafted into the service and afforded more opportunities for maturation through socialization. He was assigned to ward J1.

<u>December 8, 1957</u> by Dr. Bayley

Interpretation of chest x-ray taken on 11-26-57 is as follows:

    No significant pathology of the heart, lungs or bony thorax.

<u>December 3, 1957</u> by Dr. Bayley

Interpretation of GI Series done on 12-3-57 is as follows:

    No significant involvement of the esophagus, stomach or duodenum. Normal gastrointestinal motility without gastric residue at the 4 hour period. Gall bladder studies are suggested.

GEIN, Edward

November 26, 1957 by Dr. Stehle, Wisconsin Diagnostic Center

EEG No. 57-34; Age: 51; Referring Physician E. F. Schubert, M. D.;
Taken by C. Disterhoft, R.N.; Date of EEG Study November 26, 1957.

INTERPRETATION

Characteristics: Awake and drowsy record. Seconal gr. 1½ was given but
did not induce sleep. Record is primarily a tension
record. Basic frequency of 9-11/sec. No seizure discharges; no focus;
no asymmetry. Normal response to hyperventilation.

Impression: Normal awake and drowsy record from the accessible cortex.
A sleep record would be necessary for complete EEG
evaluation.

R Wamington

December 5, 1957 by Dr. Stehle, Wisconsin Diagnostic Center

EEG No. 57-35; Date of EEG Study December 5, 1957; Age 51; Referring
Physician E. F. Schubert, M. D.; Taken by C. Disterhoft, R.N.

INTERPRETATION

Characteristics: Record is a Seconal (gr. 3) induced drowsy and sleep
record. Normal sleep frequencies. No seizure
discharges; no focus; no asymmetry.

Impression: Normal drowsy and sleep record from the accessible cortex.
This record and awake and drowsy record of 11-26-57 give
no EEG evidence of cerebral dysrhythmia or epileptic discharges.

R Wamington

December 9, 1957 by Dr. Cook

Interpretation of skull x-ray taken 12-7-57 is as follows:

Boney tables are of normal thickness and density. There is no
evidence of old or recent fracture. There is no abnormal calcification
or vascularity. The pineal gland is not calcified. The sella turcica
and petrous ridges are normal. Impression normal skull.

December 9, 1957, by Dr. Schubert

Mr. Gein was interviewed on this date. He was oriented as to
place; however, he was not completely oriented as to time. He stated
that it was sometime in December of 1957 and gave as his excuse for not
knowing the particular day of the month, that he had no calendar and
had no newspapers from which to obtain the date. He stated that he
had seen me before and correctly indicated that such contact with me
had been on Ward J-1.

He immediately began speaking about the difficulty which brought
him to the institution. He rather vehemently stated that none of this
would have happened if his neighbors had shown some interest in him
and would have visited him. He stated that the only time the neighbors
came to his home was when they wanted to borrow things. He complained
about the neighbors playing "dirty deals." He applied this phrase to

299

December 9, 1957. by Dr. Schubert (continued)

business dealings that he had had with one particular neighbor who
had rented a field from him some years ago for $10.00 a year. This
neighbor paid the rent for the first year but neglected to pay the
rent for subsequent years. He claims that about five of his neighbors were constantly taking advantage of him and that they all owed
him money. He denied that he had any difficulty with the people in
Plainfield, although he said that many of them didn't appreciate the
things that he did for them.

He complained of memory deficits and more specifically with
regard to the crimes he is accused of committing. He stated that
he is unable to recall any of the details of the murder of Mrs.
Hogan and said that some of the things that they claim he said in
Madison at the Crime Laboratory were not true. He said that he is
unable to figure out how he could have had time to do everything
that they have accused him of doing. He also claims that he is not
clear on many of the details involved in the murder of Mrs. Worden.
He vaguely remembers putting a cartridge, which he found in his pocket,
in a rifle which he took from a rack in the Worden Store, but he
feels that her death was an accident because the gun must have discharged accidentally. He states that he does not remember putting
the body in his truck and driving it to his home, although he admits
that he must have been the one who did this.

His opinion of Mrs. Worden is that she was a rather disreputable
woman who was known to have a bad reputation. To illustrate this
opinion, he stated that, prior to the marriage of Mr. and Mrs. Worden,
Mr. Worden was keeping company with the daughter of a dentist and
that Mrs. Worden stole her future husband from this other woman, and
that this woman subsequently killed herself with chloroform because
of this. He denies that he blames Mrs. Worden for the girl's death,
but he also stated that he feels Mrs. Worden received her just desert
when her husband died of some blood dyscrasia and feels that this
was in the nature of a punishment for her.

Much of the interview was spent in discussing his feelings about
his mother. His mother was a very religious woman and his only description of her was that "she was good in every way." His mother
suffered two strokes, and much of his time was spent in caring for
his mother after the first stroke. He began to cry when he described
his mother's infirmities and stated that "she didn't deserve all of
her suffering." His mother's second stroke followed an argument that
a neighbor by the name of Smith had with his wife and daughter. This
man Smith was "an evil man" who brought a married woman to live with
him on the farm neighboring the Gein property. This man would have
temper tantrums and, upon one occasion, killed a puppy because the
dog irritated him. The patient's mother suffered her second stroke
shortly after an argument which this man had with his wife and

<u>December 9, 1957</u>, by Dr. Schubert (concluded)

daughter, and the patient feels that this man was, therefore, responsible for his mother's death.

His feelings for his father are completely negative. He stated that his father drank excessively and would abuse both him and his brother.

Following the death of his mother in 1945, he was very depressed for about two years and it was during this time that the farm fell into disrepair. He states that he "has had spells of the blues," and that he wanted to sell the farm because of all of the unpleasant memories connected with this farm. Apparently he made some half-hearted attempts to sell this farm and stated that he planned to visit some of his relatives and eventually to settle down in the southern part of the United States with the money obtained from the sale of the farm.

With respect to his claims of memory deficits, he says that his lapses of memory started after the death of his mother. While discussing much of his symptomatology, he becomes tangential and irrelevant. When asked specifically about his interests since the death of his mother, his only answer was that he wished he could have had more contact with other people. He stated that since the death of his mother he has had feelings that things around him were unreal and at one time shortly after the death of his mother, he felt that he could raise people from the dead by will power. He also stated that he heard his mother talking to him on several occasions for about a year after she died. His mother's voice was heard while he was falling asleep and, apparently, this is in the nature of a hypnagogic hallucinatory phenomenon. He has also had dreams that his mother was with him upon occasion. He mentioned one unusual experience occurring two or three years ago in which he saw a forest with the tops of the trees missing and vultures sitting in the trees; he feels that this was more in the nature of a dream.

He feels that the death of Mrs. Worden was justified because she deserved to die, and he goes on to explain that he is actually fatalistic and that this whole sequence of events was ordained to happen.

E. F. Schubert

<u>December 11, 1957</u>, by Dr. Cerny

<u>History:</u> Patient has been aware of tumor in the left outer angle since infancy. The left vision has apparently also been poor since infancy, and this was first definitely determined by an army examination. No accidents, surgery, or other eye diseases are recalled. During the past eight years the patient has suffered from periodic headaches, at first frontal, then unilateral (usually left), accompanied by nausea and vomiting, and being relieved after the acute phase. No definite eye symptoms are noted during these attacks, aside from an additional difficulty in reading. Patient also states that he usually has some difficulty reading smaller print.

<u>December 9, 1957</u>, by Dr. Schubert (concluded)

daughter, and the patient feels that this man was, therefore, responsible for his mother's death.

His feelings for his father are completely negative. He stated that his father drank excessively and would abuse both him and his brother.

Following the death of his mother in 1945, he was very depressed for about two years and it was during this time that the farm fell into disrepair. He states that he "has had spells of the blues," and that he wanted to sell the farm because of all of the unpleasant memories connected with this farm. Apparently he made some half-hearted attempts to sell this farm and stated that he planned to visit some of his relatives and eventually to settle down in the southern part of the United States with the money obtained from the sale of the farm.

With respect to his claims of memory deficits, he says that his lapses of memory started after the death of his mother. While discussing much of his symptomatology, he becomes tangential and irrelevant. When asked specifically about his interests since the death of his mother, his only answer was that he wished he could have had more contact with other people. He stated that since the death of his mother he has had feelings that things around him were unreal and at one time, shortly after the death of the mother, he felt that he could raise people from the dead by will power. He also stated that he heard his mother talking to him on several occasions for about a year after she died. His mother's voice was heard while he was falling asleep and, apparently, this is in the nature of a hypnagogic hallucinatory phenomenon. He has also had dreams that his mother was with him upon occasion. He mentioned one unusual experience occurring two or three years ago in which he saw a forest with the tops of the trees missing and vultures sitting in the trees; he feels that this was more in the nature of a dream.

He feels that the death of Mrs. Worden was justified because she deserved to die, and he goes on to explain that he is actually fatalistic and that this whole sequence of events was ordained to happen.

E. F. Schubert

<u>December 11, 1957</u>, by Dr. Cerny

<u>History:</u> Patient has been aware of tumor in the left outer angle since infancy. The left vision has apparently also been poor since infancy, and this was first definitely determined by an army examination. No accidents, surgery, or other eye diseases are recalled. During the past eight years the patient has suffered from periodic headaches, at first frontal, then unilateral (usually left), accompanied by nausea and vomiting, and being relieved after the acute phase. No definite eye symptoms are noted during these attacks, aside from an additional difficulty in reading. Patient also states that he usually has some difficulty reading smaller print.

<u>December 11, 1957</u>, by Dr. Cerny (concluded)

<u>EXAMINATION</u>:

RV 20/20 correctible to 20/15 - 2   (-.25)
LV 20/200 correctible to 20/70 - (fleetingly) $(-1.00 + 75 \text{ c } 90°)$
         central scotoma is evident, and left vision
         is slightly eccentric.

In the left outer canthus is a soft grey-pink mass, easily
visible on "eyes right". A small subcutaneous fullness is noted
at this outer angle also.
Lids and conjunctivae otherwise normal. Lacrimal apparatus neg.
E.O.M. full and parallel, in all planes, with no evidence of paresis.
Rt. pupil 4 mm. regular and active.
Left pupil 4 x 3.5 mm. slightly irregular, but active.
Cornea and anterior chamber clear.
Media clear.   Tactile Tension normal.

<u>Fundi</u>: Normal. No edema. Discs clear and healthy. No vascular
        sclerosis or other changes. No hemorrhage, congestion,
        deposits, etc. Maculae very normal.

Confrontation fields full.

<u>Diagnosis</u>: Amblyopia, left eye, congenital.
            Compound myopic astigmatism, left eye.
            Myopia, slight, right eye.
            Presbyopia.
            Lipoma or dermo-lipoma, left lateral orbit.

F. J. Cerny, M.D.

<u>December 12, 1957</u>, by Dr. Schubert

The patient was interviewed on this date. He again denied any
knowledge about the death of Mrs. Hogan and stated that he had admitted this crime because this was what the investigators wished him
to do. It was impossible to obtain a chronological series of events
with regard to the death of Mrs. Worden. He specifically denied
remembering the evisceration of the body. He stated that he had
violated nine graves and when questioned as to his reasons for doing
this, he stated that he thought it was because he wanted a remem-
brance of his mother. He denied any sexual relations with any of
these bodies and gave as his reason for this, that " they smelled
too bad." He again admitted that, for a period of time after his
mother's death, he felt that he could arouse the dead by an act of
will power. He claimed to have tried to arouse his dead mother by
an act of will power and was disappointed when he was unsuccessful.
He also admitted that he had attempted this sort of thing with

December 12, 1957, by Dr. Schubert (concluded)

some of the bodies which he had exhumed.

Questioning this man requires a great deal of tact because he is extremely suggestible and will almost invariably agree to any leading questions.

At the present time, he is in contact with his surroundings and co-operates as completely as possible. His knowledge of current events is intact and his memory for past events, with the exception of details involved in the evisceration of Mrs. Worden and the death of Mrs. Hogan, is also intact. He denies any hallucinatory phenomena at this time. There is ample reason to believe that his violation of the graves was in response to the demands of his fantasy life, which was motivated by his abnormally magnified attachment to the mother.

E. F. Schubert

December 13, 1957 by Dr. Warmington

MENTAL EXAMINATION

Personal and Family History: This patient was admitted to this institution on November 23, 1957 for a 30 day observation period under W.S.S. 957.27 (3) after he had been arrested and charged with the crime of Murder, 1st Degree. The offense occurred at Plainfield, Wisconsin on or about November 16, 1957 and involved the shooting of a woman, one Mrs. Worden, by the patient. Gein had entered a hardware store which the victim operated sometime during the morning of November 16th (?), looked over the guns, took one from a rack, found he had a .22 caliber bullet in his pocket, placed it in the gun and shot the woman in the head. The bullet apparently struck her obliquely and passed through the skull. He then walked over to her and pulled the body into a back room where it would not be visible from the street. At this time he declares he was nervous, agitated and did not think clearly but put the body in her truck which was standing in back of the store, drove it some distance, abandoned the truck, walked back to the town of Plainfield, got his car, drove to the truck and put the body in his own car. The body was then taken by him to his home and according to reports was strung up by the feet, disembowelled and mutilated. Toward evening he was taken into custody as a suspect since people had seen his car earlier in the day parked in front of the hardware store and had also seen him driving the truck. It appears that he confessed to the homicide and investigation of his house revealed several so-called human masks, the use of human skin as upholstery material for a chair and other remains of human anatomy. These findings prompted a further search of the property and several human bones and dismembered parts were excavated. According to the records, the subject confessed to the murder and admitted exhuming several whole bodies and parts of others, particularly the head and neck. Before coming here he was subjected to interrogation by authorities, was given lie detector tests and revealed his actions. Personal history reveals that the patient was born on August 8, 1906 at La Crosse, Wisconsin, spent a short

December 13, 1957 continued

time there with his parents and then moved to the Plainfield area
where they lived on a farm. In addition to the patient there was
one other male child in the family who lost his life in a fire in
1944. Edward attended a country school, attained the 8th grade
and did odd jobs, farm work and baby sitting after leaving school.
He had no technical education but describes himself as being interested in study and read considerably. Since childhood his attachment was closer to the mother than the father as the latter drank
in earlier years and seems to have been a threat to both the
mother and the patient at times. The father preceded the mother in
death and at the time of arrest Gein was living alone as the mother
had died in a hospital from a second stroke. The first stroke
occurred sometime previously and resulted in her incapacitation
and the patient's occupation with her nursing needs. He believes
that the stroke may have been precipatated by witnessing of neighbor argumentation and disturbances particularly in connection
with the first stroke and in his mind she suffered a further set-
back after the death of her elder son. In recent years he has been
a lonely individual that occasionally had some visitors to his home
and did baby sitting in the area but did not have the ordinary
social outlets.

Personality Makeup: The subject is an introverted, odd, withdrawn
personality that has had difficulty relating
closely to other people. He also has shown some paranoid trends
but on the other hand may have been duped and unfairly used on
some occasions as he speaks of doing work for other farmers and
failing to be paid for his labor. He is passive, inhibited and somewhat evasive when questioned about the offense and may harbor deep
seated feelings of hostility. He denies ever having had sexual
experience and declares that in this connection he was taught
the moral code by his mother that sexual experience before marriage
was wrong--"If a woman is good enough for intercourse, she is good
enough for marriage". In his general reaction immaturity and shy-
ness are noted, however, a certain cleverness and ability to plan
are present. A belief in spirits is also expressed by him and he
tends to be superstitious.

Mental Status: Since coming here the patient has been very tract-
able, cooperative and readily abides by the institution
rules. During sessions he sat quietly and displayed no belligerency
but information was volunteered and he discussed his case but when
interrogated for details became cloudy, cried or gave indication
that the subject was distasteful. He has been clean in personal
habits and shows no particular mannerisms or stereotypy of speech
or action. He has slept considerable and relates this to his
inability to procure uninterrupted rest prior to his hospitalization

December 13, 1957 continued

here. Consciousness is clear, there is no history of epileptic seizures,
orientation is correct in all fields and the train of thought is coherent
and relevant but sometimes somewhat illogical. Faces have been seen
by him in leaves and he spoke of hearing his mother's voice while in
a twilight sleep zone but it is uncertain if these should be designated
as overt hallucinations. No delusional material has been elicited but
his behavior has been very unusual as he admits to excavating several
bodies as mentioned above. In this connection he is not always clear
in his statements and at times holds his head and declares he is not
sure of his actions. During interviews he talked of using a rod to
determine the nature of the rough box by its sound upon tapping and
also knew some of the exhumed people in life. They were all women of
varying ages. The bodies were removed from three cemeteries--Plainfield,
Spiritland and Hancock, but some were returned after a short time as
he became remorseful. In other instances he made the so-called masks
from the head by removing the skin and separating it from the bones.
The tissue in the back of the neck was cut and the cavity stuffed with
paper or sawdust. One of these was placed in a cellophane bag but
others were kept throughout the house. The unused parts of bodies
were burned or buried and eating is denied. He has also denied having
sex relations with the bodies or parts of them as he declares the
odor was offensive. His memory is intact for most subjects but when
emotionally charged situations are encountered there is a suggestion
of a self-serving amnesia or vagueness. Denial or inability to recall
shooting Mrs. Hogan is made and there is an intimation that the most
recent homicide may have been accidental. At times the remark was made-
--"It seems like a dream, impossible". Since the death of his mother
he had feelings that things were unreal, he felt that he could raise
people from the dead by will power and some ambiguity was noted in
his account of the happenings. Mrs. Worden on one interview was described as being short, inconsiderate and brusque but during a later
interview was declared to be a friendly, pleasant woman. Physical
attraction for either woman was not admitted and he denied seriously
attempting to escort Mrs. Worden to a roller skating rink. Mrs. Hogan
was a tavern operator and it is gathered that she was regarded by the
patient as being a rather poor representative of womankind and he could
have felt justified in shooting her because of his self-righteous,
rigid attitude.

Criminal Motivation Factors and Psychodynamics: The motivation is elu-
                                                  sive and uncertain
but several factors come to mind--hostility; sex; and a desire for a
substitute for his mother in the form of a replica or body that could
be kept indefinitely. He has spoken of the bodies as being like dolls
and a certain comfort was received from their presence although ambi-
valent feelings in this regard probably occurred. When questioned
regarding the reason for his bizarre conduct, no explanation is given
but sex relations with the bodies has been denied several times. This
does not seem to check with heresay in which he admitted having sex
activities with the cadavers. He has been a lonely man particularly
since the death of his mother and some drive, uncertain at this time,
may have arisen in this area to account for his misconduct. Review of
the life of this individual indicates poor ego structure, excessive
self-consciousness and deep seated feelings of insecurity in his social

December 13, 1957 continued

contacts. The source of the poor ego strength is problematic but could be related to psychologic traumatization suffered at the hands of the father, over-identification with the mother and morphologic factors of small stature and an eye defect.

Summary: This is the case of a 51 year old, single, well developed, well nourished, white male that was admitted to this institution on November 23, 1957 for a 30 day observation period upon order of the Circuit Court of Waushara County after he had been arrested and charged with the crime of Murder, 1st Degree. He has been involved in morbid, ghoulish behavior with exhumation of several bodies and the fashioning of masks from the heads. He has also admitted to commission of the homicide in the case of Mrs. Worden but intimates that this may have been accidental and now is uncertain about his connection with another homicide that occurred a few years ago in which he has also been implicated. Longitudinal history discloses that this individual has been withdrawn, limited in his contacts over a period of years and failed to develop emotionally in a normal manner. He was overly attached to the mother and developed a diffident, non-assertive personality with consequent feelings of frustration and some hostility. Most likely particularly disturbed were sexual emotions but he is also unstable, cries easily and displays some feminine characteristics. He is intellectually adequate as shown by an I.Q. of 99 and has an average fund of school and general knowledge. Consciousness is clear, orientation is satisfactory and his verbalizations are coherent but he makes remarks suggesting a simple or primitive belief in spirits. He also probably fantasies excessively and may have been hallucinated on some occasions. His judgment has manifestly been poor and insight is faulty. Physical examination and laboratory studies are non-contributory except as related in a general sense to his personality structure.

                                        M.D.
                           Chief of Medical Services

December 18, 1957, by Staff

The members of the staff were Dr. E. F. Schubert, Dr. R. Warmington, Dr. O. Larimore, Dr. O. Goetsch, Dr. L. J. Ganser, Dr. H. J. Colgan; Mr. K. Colwell, Social Worker; and Mr. R. Ellsworth, Psychologist.

The patient was seen by the staff on this date for diagnosis. A lengthy period of questioning was conducted in which each of the staff members took part. It was determined through this questioning that the patient had been living a withdrawn and solitary existence for a number of years and, since the death of his mother in 1945, has

December 18, 1957, by Staff (continued)

had little social contact with the people in his community. His description of his mother was that she was as good a woman as it was possible for anyone to be, and through her teachings he developed a rigid moralistic attitude regarding women and the use of alcoholic beverages. He claimed to have been instructed by his mother that women in general were tainted with evil and should be shunned as much as possible. His attitude towards the drinking of alcoholic beverages was determined by his unpleasant experiences with an alcoholic father.

There was a very marked sexual pre-occupation throughout most of his answers to questions. When asked what was responsible for his activities, he stated that it was all due to "a force built up in me." He feels that this force was in the nature of an evil spirit which influenced him to dig up graves.

With respect to the charge which brought him to the institution, namely, the death of Mrs. Worden, he stated that he had been chosen as an instrument of God in carrying out what fate had ordained should happen to this woman. He stated that it would not have happened if events had not fallen into place the way they did. He placed the ultimate blame for everything that occurred on an outside force which is conceived of by him as God.

There were numerous complaints of physical illness. He complained of headaches, sore throat, chest pain, abdominal distress, and constipation. It was felt by the staff that this symptomatology could best be classified as a pseudoneurotic schizophrenic process.

He readily admitted that he had heard his mother's voice telling him to be good several years after her death and that, on one occasion, he had experienced what was probably an olfactory hallucination, in that he smelled what he thought was decaying flesh in the surrounding environment of his property. Upon occasion, he stated that he has seen faces in piles of leaves. It could not be determined whether this was actually hallucinatory phenomena or an illusion.

It was the consensus of the staff's opinion that this man is best diagnosed as a "schizophrenic reaction of the chronic undifferentiated type" and that this has been a process going on for an undetermined number of years. Because his judgment is so influenced by his envelopment in a world of fantasy, he is not considered to know the difference between right and wrong. His concept of the nature of his acts is markedly influenced by the existence of the delusional material concerned in particular with the idea that outside forces are responsible for what occurred. Because of his

December 18, 1957, by Staff (continued)

had little social contact with the people in his community. His description of his mother was that she was as good a woman as it was possible for anyone to be, and through her teachings he developed a rigid moralistic attitude regarding women and the use of alcoholic beverages. He claimed to have been instructed by his mother that women in general were tainted with evil and should be shunned as much as possible. His attitude towards the drinking of alcoholic beverages was determined by his unpleasant experiences with an alcoholic father.

There was a very marked sexual pre-occupation throughout most of his answers to questions. When asked what was responsible for his activities, he stated that it was all due to "a force built up in me." He feels that this force was in the nature of an evil spirit which influenced him to dig up graves.

With respect to the charge which brought him to the institution, namely, the death of Mrs. Worden, he stated that he had been chosen as an instrument of God in carrying out what fate had ordained should happen to this woman. He stated that it would not have happened if events had not fallen into place the way they did. He placed the ultimate blame for everything that occurred on an outside force which is conceived of by him as God.

There were numerous complaints of physical illness. He complained of headaches, sore throat, chest pain, abdominal distress, and constipation. It was felt by the staff that this symptomatology could best be classified as a pseudoneurotic schizophrenic process.

He readily admitted that he had heard his mother's voice telling him to be good several years after her death and that, on one occasion, he had experienced what was probably an olfactory hallucination, in that he smelled what he thought was decaying flesh in the surrounding environment of his property. Upon occasion, he stated that he has seen faces in piles of leaves. It could not be determined whether this was actually hallucinatory phenomena or an illusion.

It was the consensus of the staff's opinion that this man is best diagnosed as a "schizophrenia, reaction process going on for an undetermined number of years. Because his judgment is so influenced by his envelopment in a world of fantasy, he is not considered to know the difference between right and wrong. His concept of the nature of his acts is markedly influenced by the existence of the delusional material concerned in particular with the idea that outside forces are responsible for what occurred. Because of his

December 18, 1957, by Staff (concluded)

extreme suggestibility, he is not completely or fully capable of
acting in his own behalf or in consultation with his attorney.
This man, in the opinion of the staff, is legally insane and not
competent to stand trial at this time. His commitment to Central
State Hospital under Section 957.13 of the Wisconsin statutes is
recommended.

E. F. Schubert, M. D.
Superintendent

R. Warmington, M. D.
Chief of Medical Services

O. M. Larimore, M. D.
Psychiatrist

O. Goetsch, M. D.
Physician

WISCONSIN STATE BOARD OF HEALTH
ORIGINAL CERTIFICATE OF DEATH

State Filing Date

1. PLACE OF DEATH			2. USUAL RESIDENCE (Where deceased lived. If institution: residence before admission)
a. COUNTY Waushara			a. STATE Wisconsin	b. COUNTY Waushara
b. CITY (If outside corporate limits, write RURAL and give township) OR TOWN Plainfield	c. LENGTH OF STAY (in this place)		c. CITY (If outside corporate limits, write RURAL and give township) OR TOWN Plainfield
d. FULL NAME OF HOSPITAL OR INSTITUTION (If not in hospital or institution, give street address or location)			d. STREET ADDRESS (If rural, give location)

3. NAME OF DECEASED (Type or Print) a. (First) Bernice	b. (Middle) Conover	c. (Last) Worden	4. DATE OF DEATH (Month) 11 (Day) 16 (Year) 1957
5. SEX Female	6. COLOR OR RACE White	7. MARRIED, NEVER MARRIED, WIDOWED, DIVORCED (Specify) Widowed	8. DATE OF BIRTH May 9, 1899	9. AGE (in years) 58	If under 1 year Months Days	If under 24 hrs Hours Min
10a. USUAL OCCUPATION (Give kind of work done during most of working life, even if retired) Hardware		10b. KIND OF BUSINESS OR INDUSTRY Hardware	11. BIRTHPLACE (State or foreign country) Canton, Illinois		12. CITIZEN of WHAT COUNTRY? U. S. A.
13. FATHER'S NAME Frank Conover			14. MOTHER'S MAIDEN NAME Agnes Putnam		
15. WAS DECEASED EVER IN U.S. ARMED FORCES? (Yes, no, or unknown) (If yes, give war or dates of service) no	16. SOCIAL SECURITY 393-14-6814	17. INFORMANT Frank Worden			

18. CAUSE OF DEATH [Enter only one cause per line for (a), (b), and (c)]	MEDICAL CERTIFICATION		Interval Between Onset and Death
	I. DISEASE OR CONDITION DIRECTLY LEADING TO DEATH (a) Bullet wound, penetrating, skull with hemorrhage into the ventricles.		10 min.
*This does not mean the mode of dying such as heart failure, asthenia, etc. It means the disease, injury, or complication which caused death.	ANTECEDENT CAUSES Morbid conditions, if any, giving rise to the above cause (a) stating the underlying cause last DUE TO (b)		
	DUE TO (c)		
	II. OTHER SIGNIFICANT CONDITIONS Conditions contributing to the death but not related to the disease or condition causing death		
19a. DATE OF OPERATION	19b. MAJOR FINDINGS OF OPERATION		

21a. ACCIDENT SUICIDE HOMICIDE (Specify) Homicide	21b. PLACE OF INJURY (e.g. in or about home, farm, factory, street, office bldg., etc.) in her store	21c. (CITY, TOWN, OR TOWNSHIP) Village, Plainfield (COUNTY) Waushara (STATE) Wis.	20. AUTOPSY? Yes ☒ No ☐
21d. TIME (Month) (Day) (Year) (Hour) OF INJURY 11-16-57 9AM	21e. INJURY OCCURRED While at Work ☐ Not While At Work ☒	21f. HOW DID INJURY OCCUR? shot by thief.	
22. I hereby certify that I attended the deceased from _____ 19___, died on _____ 19___, and that death occurred at 9:__ m. from the cause and on the date stated above. 19___ to _____ 19___, that I last saw the deceased			
23a. SIGNATURE R. C. [signature] M. D.	(Degree or title)	23b. ADDRESS Wautoma,	23c. DATE SIGNED 11-18-57

24a. BURIAL, CREMATION, REMOVAL (Specify) Burial	24b. DATE 11-20-57	24c. NAME OF CEMETERY OR CREMATORY Plainfield,	24d. LOCATION (City, town or county) Plainfield, Wisconsin.
DATE REC'D BY LOCAL REGISTRAR 11/26/57	REGISTRAR'S SIGNATURE Carn Bunche	25. FUNERAL DIRECTOR [signature]	ADDRESS Plainfield, Wisc.

CERTIFICATE OF COMMITMENT (957.11(3), Wis. Stats.) Form MH
_____

_____

STATE OF WISCONSIN, __WAUSHARA__ COUNTY, __WAUSHARA COUNTY__ COURT

The State of Wisconsin,

                    Plaintiff, CERTIFICATE OF COMMITMENT
                       UPON ACQUITTAL BECAUSE OF
  vs.   INSANITY xxxxxxxxxxxxxxxxxx

__Edward Gein__   , Defendant, CASE NO.   __462__

    As Clerk of said Court, I hereby certify that the defendant was
tried on a charge of **feloniously and with intent to kill, murder**
Bernice Worden, a human being

CIRCUIT COURT
WAUSHARA CO., WIS.
FILED
NOV 1 4 1968
INA T. McCOMB, Clerk

in violation of Section __940.01__

Wisconsin Statutes; that at a term of Court, the Honorable
__R.H.Gollmar__ ,judge presiding, held at the Courthouse in the city
of __Wautoma, Wisconsin__   on __November 7, 1968__   ,
the defendant was found and adjudged not guilty because(insane)
(~~feebleminded~~) at the time of the commission of the offense charged;
and that upon said adjudication the Court, did on __Nov. 14,1968__ commit
the defendant under Section 957.11 (3) of the Statutes, as follows:

    "You are hereby committed to the (Central)(xxxxxxxxx) State
Hospital/__for the Criminally Insane__ ,or such other Institution as they may send
__at Waupun, Wisconsin__ ,there to be detained until discharged him
                                            to
in accordance with law, or until further order of the Court. The
Sheriff of this County shall forthwith convey you to said hospital
and place you in the custody of the Superintendent thereof and the
Superintendent shall receive you and keep you as herin ordered."

    Legal settlement of the defendant was determined to be
(__Waushara__   County) xxxxxxxxxxxxxxx).

    Given under my hand and the seal of said Court this __14th.__ day
of __November__   , 19__68__ .

                                   Ina T. McComb
                                     Clerk

THE UNIVERSITY OF WISCONSIN
MEDICAL SCHOOL
1300 UNIVERSITY AVENUE
MADISON 53706

DEPARTMENT OF PSYCHIATRY

December 6, 1973

The Honorable Robert H. Gollmar
Reserve Judge, Criminal Court Branches
2nd Judicial Circuit, Room 409
Courthouse
Milwaukee, Wisconsin 53233

Re: State of Wisconsin vs.
     Edward Gein

Dear Judge Gollmar:

Pursuant to your court order of February 26, 1973, Edward Gein, a Central State Hospital patient and petitioner for release, was examined at the hospital on March 13 and 31, April 14 and 27, and June 30, 1973 by Dr. Roberts and on March 3, 17 and 31 and June 2, 19 and 30, 1973 by Dr. Arndt. Available to us were psychological test results by Dr. Burton Michelson performed on March 19, 1973, preliminary hearing and trial transcripts and Central State Hospital records. The examination was conducted to evaluate the present mental condition of Mr. Gein in relation to possible discharge or release from Central State Hospital without danger to himself or others.

Edward Gein, born August 28, 1906, now age 66, was born in La Crosse, Wisconsin to George Gein, 31, and Augusta Loehrke Gein, 25, as the younger of two sons. A maternal uncle, Henry Loehrke, continues to reside in Grantsburg. Both parents died when Mr. Gein was in his thirties. Father was born in Coon Valley, Wisconsin and was reared after age three by Scotch maternal grandparents after his parents and sisters drowned in a flood. Following his elementary school education he began work shoeing horses as a blacksmith's helper. He later worked in La Crosse where he met his future wife. Following marriage when he was 24 and she 18, their two sons were born in La Crosse two and seven years later. The family was limited in economic ability as father worked selling insurance, in a tannery and at the city power house. The marriage and family relationships are described as normal -- "There's no perfect marriage". In 1913 father bought and worked a dairy farm, with added crop cultivation, in the lowlands near Camp Douglas. He traded it for a similar type farm near Plainfield in 1914 and Edward Gein spent the rest of childhood and adulthood from age eight ___ ___ ___ Father is described in the ___ ___ ___ ___ ___ to his sons. It is also Mr. Gein who calls father hard working. The two statements are now denied by years before his 1940 death at age 65. Father was a cardiac invalid 1-1/2

313

Mother, of German ancestry, was the family decision maker, dominant parent and at times she did the family farm work. Mother's parents were immigrants from Germany who married before coming to the U.S. Maternal grandfather farmed just outside La Crosse. Mother was a plump pleasant person who spoke both German and English at home. Mr. Gein felt very close to her and accepted her guidance and demands. He described her as thrifty, hard working and a moralistic religious person. She could make others feel better and enjoyed life. She treated her two sons equally and taught them to behave properly. She had heart problems for a number of years before having a stroke. She remained non-complaining with gradual recovery at home after initial hospitalization. Mr. Gein provided nursing care and ambulation assistance for her. A second stroke a few weeks after her oldest son's death and shortly after an argument with a neighbor proved fatal at age 64 in 1945.

His brother, Henry George Gein, was born in 1901, five years before Edward's arrival. He had an elementary school education before working as a farmer. He remained a bachelor and was one of several male family members on mother's side of the family who never married. As children the two boys had average closeness considering their age difference. Both enjoyed trout fishing with father. In addition to work on the family farm Henry worked for neighboring farmers, for a road building contractor and a power and light utility company setting poles and stringing wires to supplement family income. With some pride Edward speaks of his brother's ability to direct and control a crew of Jamaican farm workers as their foreman during World War II. Others had greater difficulty in that task.

From the description, mother was the strong force in this family of three men. Father's death in 1940 removed a source of family problem but father was also a central pillar of the family unit. Henry then died in 1944 at 43 in a marsh fire. The involvement of Edward in this blaze with psychological "What if I had ___?" guilt implications and the death of mother not too long after left Edward very isolated and deeply emotionally traumatized. The two men were burning off a marsh and during a temporary absence of Edward the blaze got out of control asphyxiating his brother. It was several hours before his body was found by a search party with Edward guiding them to the site. This event is tearfully related as "the start of my trouble".

This family was economically limited throughout recalled childhood and adulthood. Edward refers to them as average and normal though the description compiled between hospital records and his comments paints it differently. Marital unhappiness by mother over her husband's alcohol consumption, marginal work and abusiveness might have caused divorce were it not for her religious to mother's quarrelsome nature and intense religious beliefs with moralistic preachiness. Edward is defensive about that view of his family. A childhood recall includes fear of blood with inability to watch slaughtered animals being "dressed out". He was self taught to play three family musical instruments at home -- harmonica (father's), accordion (mother's) and violin (uncle's). He had filled in as a substitute musician on the violin and accordion playing at barn dances. This activity largely ceased after mother's death as he was "too busy".

He began school in La Crosse where he attended 1-2 years and learned to read. No school was available in Juneau County so there was an educational lapse until they moved to Waushara County. He completed the rest of his elementary education in a country school of about 12 students by age 16-17 in two different one-room schools not far from home. Relations with peers and teachers was satisfactory but there was very slight interest in girl classmates. One teacher gave dancing lessons after school. He regrets his limited formal education. He was an average student and no extracurricular activities were available. He liked to read on a wide range of subjects.

Mr. Gein remained single, virginal and little involved in heterosexual relationships throughout his life. Early sexual information came from mother as that provided by peers was regarded as uncouth. Premarital sexual abstinence was stressed and the non-marital relationships of others was considered immoral, even in need of punishment. Any female with whom he would relate needed mother's approval. He was teased about his bachelorhood by other men. He "never found the right girl" was the stated reason for staying single.

His basic vocation was farming, both self-employed and working for others for limited income. Until the invalidism and later death of nuclear family members he shared work on the family farm with them. Thereafter he entered a period of mental depression, the work became more difficult for him and progressively the farm itself deteriorated. From this 1945-47 period on he gradually sold off the livestock and increasingly worked more for others. He had earlier sold equipment to pay for his mother's funeral expenses and then bought it back at a higher price when he was able to afford it. After 1945 the farm began to reseed to woodland and he made half hearted efforts to sell it in order to move to the South after visiting other relatives. He did odd jobs, baby sitting, worked as a farm hand and was employed by the town of Plainfield part-time (1945-47). Avocational pleasures were skiing, archery, sports observation, listening to music, playing musical instruments (violin-accordion-harmonica), movies (western and adventure), reading (historical, anthropological, adventure), square dances (observe or musician but too self-conscious to dance) and hunting. Most striking through the 1945-47 period was his social isolation that influenced all other spheres of his life.

He was rejected for military service in 1942 (then age 36). He is Lutheran by religious background -- synod unknown. Much religious teaching from mother was strict and contrary to the more relaxed community religious pattern. The family attended church little after leaving La Crosse early in Edward's childhood. After mother's death he found it hard to reconcile her suffering with a loving God but he later returned to his religious belief though without affiliation with any religious institution.

Mr. Gein, a 150 pound, 67 inch tall gray haired man who appears in good health and states that he is considering his 66 years. He has a congenital

skin fold of his left eye but is otherwise not distinctive in appearance.
Past surgical procedures include a lymph node biopsy (chronic granulmatous
lymphadenitis of undetermined etiology) and right inguinal herniorrhaphy.
He has some limitation of motion in his right shoulder. Prior use of alcohol
was moderate. The granloma of his lymph nodes was considered as a possible
Boeck's sarcoid. He took INH in 1969-70 for a diffuse pulmonary granularity
with adenopathy. His hospital diagnosis since 1957 has been chronic schizophrenia.

Mr. Gein minimizes his involvement in alleged behaviors from 1947
on through the next decade by declaring amnesia for much of them. When
pressed as to events reported by others he first remains non-committal but
doesn't deny them, merely asserting he can't remember. As the interviews
progress his recall improves but he then states he is unclear as to what is
remembered from personal experience and what he was told by others. He also
states his effective therapy aided his suppression of recall of past behavior
and that he doesn't desire to increase his recall of abhorred experiences.
At times he becomes quite legalistic in explaining why someone else must have
committed the crimes rather than himself -- "How could I have started the
truck without a switch key? Why didn't the deputy sheriff find her body the
first time he came to the house? It can't be a mask if it couldn't be put on".
He then reasons some other persons committed these behaviors, not himself --
such as the man who lived across the road. If pressed further, he finally
says it must be me if others say I did it. Defensively he states that if he
were to recall these happenings it would mean he perpetrated them and therefore he was not mentally ill at the time.

He dates the onset of severe pressures in his life to about 1944. He
believes varied events would have been avoided if he had married, was
better treated by neighbors or had sold the farm and left the area. The
greatest life crisis was his mother's death. He was very lonely after her
death and tried to arouse her from death by willpower. He was very isolated
from his neighbors and other social contacts. Anger without direct expression
dominated his relationship with his neighbors since he believed his family had
treated them too well without reciprocal positive responses. Loans of wagons
and farm machinery to others were one sided and the same pattern continued
after his parents deaths. Neighbors failed to repay debts on money he loaned
to them and they engaged in "crooked" behavior by cheating the government.
Through 1944-47 he spent his time reading a great deal -- historical action
stories, of Nazi atrocities including lamp shade tattoos found at a German concentration camp ordered by a woman and South Sea island ceremonies. He learned
of head hunters and cannibals as well as of those who shrink heads and make
death masks. One recalled adventure focused on a man who killed another for
his yacht before he himself was captured and killed by head hunters. His reading
about events in Germany included the making of lamp shades from human skin and
of exhumation of bodies in Wisconsin and by justification for reliving those experiences
himself.

He denies recall of any exhumation and dissection of bodies. When pressed as to his earlier report of this he says "I must have done it if I said I did but I don't remember it". Earlier reporting to other physicians as described in the hospital record and court transcript included the following paraphrased reporting. Mr. Gein reportedly was motivated by hostility, diffuse sexual need and need for maternal comfort in 1947 at the time he read an obituary announcement of a middle aged woman he had known. She was obese like his mother. He felt a sense of excitment and pressure as though forced into action by an evil spirit in a preordained way as he exhumed her body the night after the funeral. Other emotions were guilt, anxiety and shame. After some body parts were removed for preservation, the body was returned to the grave. This activity was repeated about nine times later with female bodies, of varied ages. He had known most of these persons before their burial in the three cemetaries in the Plainfield, Wisconsin area. Though sexual excitement was involved there was no sexual behavior with the bodies which smelled offensively. Skin from heads with long hair and sexual organs (breasts and genitalia) were especially preserved in cellophane bags. No human flesh was eaten nor was any body chosen because of its physical attractiveness. He recalls words from Solomon in the Bible about consumption of flesh and wondered if it referred to cannibalism. The actions sound compulsive in their ritualistic destructive handling. He denies use of special instruments or possession of anatomical books to aid in this process. The behaviors were apparently comforting, relieving of internal pressures and done with a kind of reverence as he handled the objects sought as a type of trophy. His needs later changed and the activity reportedly ceased after 1952. His marked isolation prevented discovery of this activity though he retained the objects in his home through succeeding years.

Another event with which he is linked in the records, though never charged as a crime, is the murder of Mary Hogan which he denied at this time to Dr. Roberts. She was a tavern keeper in Pine Grove, Portage County when reportedly killed in December, 1954. Mr. Gein knew her from stopping in her tavern but suspects other men must have caused the death of this foul-tongued woman. He acknowledges physical evidence caused him to be suspected of her death and hints her death may have been no great loss. To Drs. Arndt and Mickelson he stated that he had killed Mary Hogan.

One crime he admits is causing the death of Mrs. Bernice Worden by gunshot wound on Saturday, November 16, 1957. A motivating factor cited is her need for punishment with himself as a preordained divine instrument in this behavior. She took her husband from a married woman who suicided by inhalation of chloroform. She allegedly broke up another marriage earlier. Mr. Gein viewed her husband's death by a blood dyscrasia as his just reward. He also describes as motivating factors in his behavior his isolation and failure of neighbors to treat him fairly, such as repaying their debts to him. Religious justification, isolation and anger built on rejection stand out as reasons behind his action though he believes it may have been an accidental shooting, saying he was not familiar with that specific gun's action.

That November, 1957 day started out in an ordinary way as he arose about 6:00 A.M., prepared and ate breakfast and washed the dishes. It was a rainy day on which he drove his car 6-1/2 miles to Plainfield. He purchased kerosene,

317

placed in his container, for use in his kerosene stove and lamps, from a gas station at the edge of town. He then went to the Worden Hardware Store to purchase antifreeze to be placed in a glass container he had taken with him. He had obtained two gallons of antifreeze from them one week earlier. The store, previously owned by her husband and father, was managed by Mrs. Worden and her son, Frank. Mr. Gein had known her a long time and teased her one or two years earlier about going out roller skating with her. He denied knowing her well, thinking about her or having any sexual interest in her. Most of his shopping for items of the type sold in that store was done in Wisconsin Rapids. He paid for his purchase and took it to his car. He then returned to the store to look at a rifle he considered purchasing, in trade for one of his own. After asking permission and receiving it from her, he removed the rifle from under the chain holding it in a display rack. Mrs. Worden was standing one aisle away with her back to him watching deer hunters across the street bring in a deer killed on the first day of the hunting season. He took a shell from his pocket and placed it in the gun. As he checked the slide action of the gun, different than the bolt action to which he was accustomed, the weapon discharged. The victim fell to the floor dead, shot through the head. He doesn't recall aiming the gun. He agitatedly went to her and touched her. He recalls dragging her body through the store to place it in her pickup truck in the rear. Further recall for several hours is now denied. He earlier, based on available records, told how he drove the truck away, exchanged it for his car in which he took the body home and dissected it. The body was found decapitated, disembowled and strung up by the heels in the rear of his farm house that evening. He recalls talking with deer hunters at home before conversing with an adolescent neighbor girl, Darlene Hill, who stopped by with her two younger brothers. He reponded to their father's request relayed by Darlene for aid with their car trouble by getting a car battery for him at the Gamble Store in Plainfield. He returned to the Hill residence in W. Plainfield for lunch and was apprehended there for questioning about the murder before being taken to jail in Wautoma.

He was charged with first degree murder and returned to Central State Hospital in January, 1958 as incompetent to stand trial after a six week examination there. He felt abused in the initial questioning and the evaluation. His first request was for prison incarceration rather than staying in the hospital but he is now reconciled to the latter. An electroencephalogram was normal as he began his hospital stay. During this time his home was burned in the Spring of 1958 and his property sold, leaving him only future funeral expenses with the balance of the money retained by the state. Initially he was passive and developed somatic symptoms in the hospital but these subsided after one year. He worked several years as a hospital orderly, caring for other patients, and several more as an occupational therapy aide. In the latter position he did rug weaving, then lapidary and jewelry making. After ten years he returned to court as competent to stand trial and was tried later that year. In November, 1968 he was found not guilty by reason of insanity and returned to the hospital where he has remained since. He has worked successively at office cleaning, masonry and carpentry work. He is not receiving tranquilizing medication and adjusts well on one of the highest privilege hospital wards. He works daily, attends church, is polite and conforming. The hospital treatment has been satisfactory and fair, he states, but he now desires to live outside the institution. Earlier plans to go to Australia are less discussed at this time. He has also talked of manufacturing some devices he hopes to invent, such as odor removing devices by special venting in toilets. He has no visitors and little mail. One concern about the hospital is his belief that formerly strict discipline has become too lax.

Mr. Gein has now been evaluated by a number of mental health professionals over the past 15 years and spent nearly all of that time in a mental hospital. As a consequence his present appearance to the examiners is highly colored by that fact and by his desire to appear in good health, non-dangerous and ready to be discharged by the court. He is now a self-contained, quiet reserved man who desires to reveal little of himself. Thus, the examiner must use inference and observation in making the evaluation.

Mr. Gein is pleasant but wary on initial contact. He acknowledges understanding the nature of the evaluation, its purpose and its non-confidentia nature. His appearance is average, not bizarre or striking -- about what would be expected for a man in his sixties who spent his life as a central Wisconsin farmer in an isolated manner. There is nothing superficially about him to mark him as unusual. His step is active, his movements coordinated, his mind alert, his speech and manner pleasant but overcontrolled. He enjoys watching women walk and stares at them making friendly, superficial, favorable comments to or about them to others currently near him. He readily discusses his activity of the day, the state of the weather and attempts to always keep the conversation focused on appropriate ideas and feelings. This is his overt appearance. Mr. Gein is a man of average intelligence, whose formal education limitations have reduced full development of his potentials. Similarly his pattern of restricting his life experience, past and present in a psychological sense, limit his intellectual development, as does his emotional disturbance. Considering the foregoing he has an average fund of general information. His intelligence was measured in 1957 on WAIS test as an I.Q. of 99 full scale, 89 performance scale and 106 verbal. Present intelligence appears similar to that measured level.

He is oriented as to time, place and person and his judgement for handling abstract theoretical situations, detached from the events, is appropriate. Tha is, in response to questioning about an appropriate response to a given life situation, he reports what most others would do. He can also generalize in his thinking from the specific detailed elements to demonstrate his capacity for abstract thinking. His reports of memory vary widely -- from precise detail, repetitively reported in the same manner, of events occurring much earlier in his life, to accurate rapid recital of current activities and experiences and to gross gaps in information now unrecalled but previously reported. It is clear on talking with him that his recall for the latter events is highly dependent on his desire to share it, on his view of a correct relationship with the examiner, on his unwillingness to see himself objectively in relation to the information and on possible consequences of sharing it. Thus his memory appears uneven and variable in his reporting and these factors appear to accoun for better recall at one time than another. His desire to be amnesic is evident, but we believe it is partly feigned, partly a psychological defensive process and somewhat caused by the limits on his memory by limited recording and erosion by the passage of time when confronted by examiners he reveals anger, a display of temper and projects some hostility. Recent memory is good. The pattern described was noted in 1957 but is more pronounced now. His vocabulary is good. No psychological test or clinical findings indicate evidence of organic brain difficulty other than usual expected decrements with aging.

Mr. Gein desires to see himself as confirming, likeable, creative, just and of average to above average ability as a person. It has been hard for him to match that with his life experience, his treatment by others and his limited interpersonal and vocational successes. He functioned adequately, but with limited risk-taking and success, through 38 years with his mother. His life had structure and meaning which collapsed with the successive losses of father, brother and mother. Though not close emotionally as conventionally viewed nonetheless the ties of each to the other were inextricably supporting and sustaining while the outer world of people were seen as hostile, selfish and unrewarding. It was into the latter environment he was fully thrust in 1945 with resultant deterioration of his farming capability, with no person to be loved or loved by, interested or interested in, and as victim of his own psychological processes and fantasies.

He can sustain conventional, consensually accepted, patterns of thinking as long as he focuses on this and is not under much stress. As stress increases his thinking becomes tangential to an initial central idea and then alogical. The greater the emotional stimulus causing this stress the less he remains in contact with a reality shared by others. In such situations it requires increasing constant conscious effort to keep in contact with reality and to conform with other's expectations. One means of handling this is through an active fantasy life. This was especially noted in 1957 and less since then. A female identification was prominent then, with earlier ideas of transsexual surgical change on which he never followed through. The related behaviors with female body parts which were preserved has not been fully explained since he doesn't discuss this now. In fantasy he is more capable than in life -- an inventor for example.

His thinking processes have been unusual at varied times -- seeing faces in the leaves on the ground at the hospital, having visions of life before he was born, and belief in his power to raise others from the dead, particularly his mother. The year or two after her death was very traumatic, with severe depression, withdrawal, nightmares, hypnogogic hallucinations of mother's voice and social isolation. He felt things about him were unreal *and that life events, including his later behavior, was preordained to* happen. It is part of a basic belief in superstition. He then developed reasons why events did occur, such as justification on grounds of justice, the action of uncontrollable outside forces or religious punishment. Sexual preoccupation, quite in contrast with his basically asexual interpersonal activity, flourished as a replacement for fulfillment of social and personal needs.

Judge Robert H. Gollmar
December 6, 1973
Page 9

Under stress his concentration becomes impaired, his speech more
rambling, the organization of his ideas less adequate and his conversation more subjectively oriented rather than shared with his listener.
In these situations he is less able to effectively use his intelligence
and maintain desired controls over thinking and behavior. All of these
are relative deficits. At no time in the interview nor in known behavior
since 1957 has he been markedly out of control or substantially out of
contact with reality. Yet the tendency for such impairment persists and
it is seen in small amounts depending on circumstances and perceived
stresses.

Emotionally the most prominent features are his insecurity, passive
dependence, self-doubt, tension, anger, suspicion and a degree of suggestibility. For the most part he is emotionally colorless with some blunting
of his emotional responses. This is countered by his desire to please
others and be accepted by them. It makes him a somewhat unreliable
historian for he may be overly agreeable to suggested responses presented
by an examiner. On the other hand his self-protective needs counter this
and keep him from disclosing himself, his ideas and emotions, as much as do
most persons. It makes for interesting contradictions in his appearance.
Another way the same phenomenon is manifest is his naivete and social
inexperience that were so prominent in 1957 are now countered by his
institution-wise appearance fifteen years later. Yet he remains quite
socially inexperienced in many life areas in terms of depth relationships.
As a result he is poorly aware of the impact of his responses and behavior
on others and poorly empathetic with them. It isn't clear that he has ever
known the sustaining impact of a continuing loving relationship with anyone
in the manner and depth known to most. This creates a void which renders
him fearful and uncertain in social relationships with a tendency to let
others take the initiative. This is covered by some awareness of socially
appropriate themes on which he talks quite well in a superficial manner.

Since our self-learning comes through a process of relating to others
and seeing ourselves reflected through them it means Mr. Gein has a low
level of self-awareness, self-understanding and even self-identity. He
seeks this through dependence on others who will like him. Early life
experience brought him closer to mother than father but her judgemental
tendencies apparently kept her at some distance from all persons. Not knowing himself better renders Mr. Gein a victim of his own behavior since under
novel or stressful situations his behavior may appear erratic and unpre-
dictable even to himself. He thus lacks a well developed ego and is immature
despite his chronological age and experience.

He is least comfortable and self-aware in his relationships with women.
He lacks assurance of a vital sense of masculinity and has been unable to
ever relate to women in a usual heterosexual manner. Despite this his needs
for acceptance and love are evident and his avoidance of such relationships
leaves him emotionally frustrated despite efforts to suppress this. He lives
with women only in a fantasied relationship with some preoccupation about this
It was especially prominent during the period following mother's death and th

few years thereafter. The lack of such relationships and the need for but absence of such heterosexual social experience has caused Mr. Gein to be unable to sort out the differences in maternal, peer, social, affectionate and sexual relationships between a male and female. He thus has been unable to meet usual types of needs in the manner available to most persons.

With his low level of self-awareness he has a low level of faith and trust in others. Trust usually begins to develop early in life but it remains a deficit for Mr. Gein. He is sufficiently apart emotionally from others that he believes life events just happen to him. In some sense they do, for he is victimized by his own responses beyond a level of self-awareness or volitional choice when under enough stress. He is also sufficiently passive that he permits others to lead, in social and interpersonal activity. His life experience has led him to be superstitious and to believe in pre-ordained pre-determined magical events for he regards much that has happened to him as out of his own self-control. He finds it hard to believe or accept that past behaviors he knows as his own and are reported to him by others are actually his. They seem to be the acts of others or caused by unknown forces acting on him and in him. He thus denies, rationalizes and minimizes such events. He tries hard to suppress knowledge of them and repeatedly states it is important for his therapy that he do so. It is part of his pattern of continuing low self-awareness and serves to keep his anxiety level reduced and overly self-controlled and self-contained.

He focuses more on specific minor details than on a total experience and can distort, as more significant aspects of given experiences are ignored or not perceived. None of these traits are able to keep the emotions of guilt and anxiety out of Mr. Gein's self-awareness. He is near tears on occasion related to his guilt and self-deprecation over past behaviors that he can scarcely acknowledge as his own as he states, "I must have done it if they say so". His tension is also evident and rises to anger on some occasions. But most of the time his emotions are subdued, constricted and blunted and he appears to live in his present environmental situation with himself and with others in relative emotional comfort maintained only by energy expended to repress primitive feelings and ideas threatening periodically to break into conscious awareness.

Another device used to maintain psychological comfort is projection of his own emotions, ideas and behavior onto others. He attributes much of the ideas and feelings that go on inside himself. Thus he sees others as angry, hurtful, unloving and destructive wherein this is his own reflected mirrored image that he sees as belonging to others. It is easy for this to happen since he doesn't know himself well and lives with a fantasied idea of self-identity which is larger than life. How much and how often he distorts his thinking in these ways and becomes angry depends on how much he is under stress. The tendency to mistrust others and to distort their reaction to him is constant. His ever present underlying anger is usually overcontrolled and well controlled. However, he is always capable of provoking anger in other persons. The entire pattern is called paranoid thinking. When paranoid he considers himself as very self-important. He thinks others persecute him because he is so powerful, that they try to influence him and that he can cause particular behaviors in others. This unreality in his thinking distorts what objectively occurs around him.

In the interviews there were several outbursts of anger when he felt pushed by the examiner. The response considerably exceeded the stimulus and provided an opportunity to observe Mr. Gein's continued lowered threshold for activating distortion of other's responses, and a resultant use of projection followed by overt anger. It is believed that in a less controlled situation than the hospital his options for maintaining emotional control would be diminished. Social withdrawal and isolation is one such pattern which leaves him prey to his own thoughts and emotional processes. Another tension reducing device is conversion of anxiety to bodily symptoms. At times in the hospital he has complained of blurred vision, headaches, dizziness and pains in his neck and abdomen. This has not been prominent in recent years but psychosomatic symptoms early in his hospital stay and later a poorly defined pulmonary illness may be manifestations of this pattern. During an earlier time he also had a severe depression and later engaged in bizarre aggressive behaviors. Thus he has several alternative directions for control of tension, with some of the patterns most useful after marked stress and others at lower stress levels.

The clinical diagnosis rendered earlier in hospitalization has been chronic schizophrenia. Its originating date was 1947, and perhaps earlier. Whether the depression in 1945 was part of the same illness is hard to be certain in retrospect but it may have been. The symptoms were moderate in intensity in 1957, much lessened but present in 1968 and about the same in 1973 as in 1968.

Mr. Gein's chronic schizophrenic illness continues despite his extended hospital treatment. Within the supportive structure of the hospital he remains in good control of his behavior. His psychological appearance continues with a range of discrepant features -- child-like openness, naivete, directness contrasted with wariness, evasion, suspicion; good intellectual capability despite the limits of formal education and life experience; suggestibility but cautious cooperative responsiveness; emotional blunting and bursts of anger, tension, sadness and humor. Assets include some of these elements plus 1) the passage of considerable time since he last exhibited either overt psychosis or bizarre destructive behavior, 2) his desire for conformity and 3) the hospital treatment he has received. He is mentally ill but not overtly psychotic at this time. Liabilities are the presence of continued illness which earlier flared into overt psychosis and his bizarre behavipr; persistent sexual preoccupation; use of projection and hostility which are adequately controlled in the hospital; the added stresses of community life were he to be released, with adjustments needed to 1) less supervision in a less structured hospital life, 2) vocational retirement, 3) hostility and possible ridicule of persons in the community; aging processes; asocial life style (both protective and stressful). He cannot face his own past behavior as he denies its recall in a manner suggesting that he can't face it. This means his past behavior continues as a problem for him. While not discussing it is useful in maintaining psychological comfort, it makes release consideration more hazardous than would otherwise be true.

The risks of dangerousness presented by his illness are very low under conditions of minimal hospital supervision. These predictions are always very difficult and the tendency is to overpredict such risks. With his past history it is not possible to say there is no risk of dangerous behavior, indeed it remains higher than the average person in the community and will always be so. Yet balancing all the factors involved this risk is very low and not such as to necessitate a continued residence in a maximum security institution. The difficulty with this consideration in the case of Mr. Gein is his high visibility and possible major consequences if he should conceivably engage in a repetition of earlier bizarre and destructive behaviors though the possibility of this while under structured supervision is remote.

In summary, Mr. Gein has partially recovered from the psychosis he had when entering the hospital. He is not "cured" since such an illness leaves residuals which continue though they are not significantly disabling in his daily living. Were he not known by history only a very thorough mental health examination would elicit these difficulties. He is desirous of leaving the present hospital and slightly knowledgeable of problems that may be faced outside the institution though it is hard for him to emotionally comprehend them. It is suggested to the court that a plan for a gradual decrease in institutional control be initiated working toward future hospital release. This could include transfer to one of the other state hospitals where less control would be maintained. In that setting added planning toward later release could be developed. It is hard to yet see full discharge without some continuing court directed supervision of Mr. Gein as in his best interest and safety or that of the community.

Thank you for the opportunity of examining Mr. Gein. We will be pleased to answer other questions in this matter as desired by the court.

Sincerely yours,

Leigh M. Roberts, M.D.
Professor & Acting Chairman

LMR/llt

George W. Arndt, M.D. Diplomat American Board of Psychiatry and Neurology
Psychiatric Consultant, State of Wis.
Department of Social Services
Division of Corrections and
Division of Mental Hygiene

RIVERSIDE CLINIC

FAMILY MEDICINE
WILLIAM B. HILDEBRAND, M.D.
INTERNAL MEDICINE
FREDRIC L. HILDEBRAND, M.D.
WILLIAM F. SICKELS, M.D.
DAVID S. HATHAWAY, M.D.
JOSEPH F. BACHMAN, M.D.
EDWARD S. SCANLAN, M.D.

PEDIATRICS
G. DOUGLAS REILLY, M.D.
HOWARD L. KIDD, M.D.
PSYCHIATRY
THOMAS J. MALUEG, M.D.
RICHARD B. STAFFORD, M.D.

GENERAL SURGERY
GEORGE P. SCHWEI, M.D.
LUIS G. CAMACHO, M.D.
THORACIC AND VASCULAR SURGERY
LUIS G. CAMACHO, M.D.

OPHTHALMOLOGY
JOHN E. CONWAY, M.D.
KENNETH G. NEWBY, M.D.
OTOLARYNGOLOGY
JOHN E. CONWAY, M.D.
UROLOGY
JOHN T. CAMPBELL, M.D.

ADMINISTRATION
JOHN G. HEINSOHN

April 25, 1974

The Honorable R.H. Gollmar
Circuit Judge
Waushara County
Wautoma, Wisconsin 54982

Dear Judge Gollmar:

RE: Edward Gein

At your request I recently performed a psychiatric evaluation of Mr. Edward Gein, having examined him at Central State Hospital on January 31, February 20, March 5, and March 12, 1974. My examination was performed with special interest in Mr. Gein's present mental condition and his ability to adjust to living outside an institutional setting.

Mr. Gein's past psychiatric history, his social history and all the events leading to his institutionalization have been thoroughly and repeatedly recorded and documented by other professionals. For that reason I will not repeat such information in this report. My own psychiatric history obtained from Mr. Gein during the previously mentioned interviews essentially concurs with that recorded by Drs. Roberts and Arndt in their recent evaluation of him.

Mental status examination of Mr. Gein revealed the following. The patient generally appears relaxed, and would present no obvious evidence of serious mental disorder to any casual observer. His attitude toward the examiner was friendly and he was willing to talk openly with me except when discussing stressful matters. He was alert and normally oriented to time, place and person. His affect was appropriate and he possessed a normal degree of emotional reactivity when discussing relatively non-threatening material. However, when asked about or directly confronted with the facts which lead to his institutionalization, he would become significantly anxious, agitated, and angry. He repeatedly made statements such as "I don't want to rake up the past. If you stir up the past you might get burnt up in your own fire. Psychiatrists are probably responsible for alot of trouble in the world because of making people dig up the past and scaring people of society. I think some of the prisoners from here might go out and kill 'em, rob 'em, club 'em up because of digging up the past." Mr. Gein's thought processes were generally intact and reasonably well organized. There was no evidence of an overt associative thought disorder of psychotic quality. Again, when stressed by discussing difficult material his thinking would become loose, disorganized, and rambling. Mr. Gein's interpretation of proverbs was very much personalized. When asked to give the meaning of "People who live in glasses houses shouldn't throw stones," he stated that "everybody has something he wants covered up." When asked to give the meaning of the proverb "Still water rungs deep" he responded saying "Some people are calm on the surface and hot heads underneath. When asked to give the meaning of the proverb "Don't cry over spilled milk" he responded by saying "Don't dig up the past--what's done is done." When asked to give the meaning of the proverb "A bird in the hand is worth two in the bush" he laughed somewhat inappropriately and said "If you have a bird in your hand you might squeeze him too much and kill him." There was no evidence of clear-cut delusional ideation but the patient's inclinations to blame other people and outside agencies for his own discomfort became readily apparent when he was anxious. There were no evidences of hallucinations or any other perceptual distortions. His memory seemed generally intact, both for recent and remote events except for an obviously psychologically induced amnesia for the crimes of which he has been convicted. Mr. Gein's amnesia represents a well developed repressive defense against overwhelming anxiety.

The patient's general fund of information was perfectly normal for his age and his circumstances. His ability to make abstract judgements seems intact and appropriate. His interpersonal relationships, by his own description, seem rather shallow. He states that he is "afraid of pressure and is not too thick with anybody." Mr. Gein has little insight concerning the possibility that society may remember him and his notoriety and may continue to respond to him in ways that could be anxiety provoking. He feels that everyone has forgotten him and that he will be able to simply walk away from harrassment should it occur. He has some unrealistic plans about going to Australia after being released although he is not certain about how to arrange for his travel plans.

In my opinion, Mr. Gein's latent schizophrenic illness could still be reactivated by the kind of stress that he would seem likely to meet should he be released. It is conceivable that he may still be a danger to himself or others under these circumstances. Since he has responded so well to life in an institutional setting I would suggest that he be transferred to a less restricted facility in order to afford him the greater degree of freedom that he wishes. I believe that Winnebago State Hospital would probably be adequate for these purposes and that some time in the foreseeable future a county hospital transfer might also be feasible.

Thank you very much for the opportunity to evaluate Mr. Gein.

Sincerely,

Thomas J. Malueg, M. D.

/jah

326

CENTRAL STATE HOSPITAL

Received of the Sheriff of .... Waushara .... County

this ..... 28th ...... day of .... June ...., 19.. 74

(name) .... Edward Gein ....

who was committed by the .... Circuit .... Court

for the County of .... Waushara ....

E.F. Schlegt

Per *Leo Copeland*

Superintendent

Central State Hospital
Waupun, Wisconsin

RO6

STATE OF WISCONSIN   CIRCUIT COURT   WAUSHARA COUNTY
- -

In the Matter of the Mental Condition of

      EDWARD GEIN   WRIT OF HABEAS CORPUS

Heretofore Adjudged to be Mentally Ill.

                                             FILED

- -

THE STATE OF WISCONSIN:

      To the Honorable E. F. Schubert, M. D., Superintendent of Central

State Hospital, Waupun, Wisconsin.

      GREETINGS:

      You are hereby commanded to have the above named patient, Edward

Gein, detained in your custody in the Central State Hospital at Waupun, as it

is said, under safe and secure conduct before said Court at the Court House

in the City of Wautoma, Wisconsin, on the 27th day of June, 1974, at 10:00

o'clock in the forenoon to appear at a re-examination conducted before the

said Court in relation to adjudgment as mentally ill and on the 26th day of

June, 1974, for conference with his attorney; and immediately after the com-

pletion of said re-examination, that you return him to the Central State

Hospital under safe and secure conduct; and have you then and there this writ.

      WITNESS: The Honorable R. H. Gollmar, Circuit Court Judge,

Wautoma, Waushara County, Wisconsin, this 19th day of June, 1974.

                                  R. H. Gollmar, Circuit Court
                                           Judge

STATE OF WISCONSIN   CIRCUIT COURT   WAUSHARA COUNTY
- -

In the Matter of the Mental Condition of

     EDWARD GEIN   ORDER GRANTING WRIT

Heretofore Adjudged to be Mentally Ill.

- -

     Upon reading and filing the petition of Robert P. Rudolph, Special
Prosecutor for the State of Wisconsin, County of Waushara, duly signed and
verified by him, whereby he applies for a Writ of Habeas Corpus, it appearing
that said patient is confined and committed to Central State Hospital at
Waupun, Wisconsin; that of the said Central State Hospital at Waupun, Wisconsin, Dr
E. F. Schubert is Superintendent; that said patient is confined and committed
as a result of having been adjudged mentally ill by the Circuit Court of
Waushara County, Wisconsin, on November 15, 1968. There is scheduled before
the said court a re-examination in relation to the patient, Edward Gein's,
mental capacity pursuant to Chapter 51 of the Wisconsin Statutes and that
the said patient shall be present at said re-examination; that said
petitioner has prayed that a Writ of Habeas Corpus be issued herein directed
to E. F. Schubert, M. D., Superintendent of the Central State Hospital,
commanding that he have the body of the patient, Edward Gein, before the
said court on the 27th day of June, 1974, so that the patient may be in
attendance at said re-examination as required by law and that the said patient
be brought to Waushara County on June 26, 1974, for the purpose of a
conference with his attorney;

     And it appearing to the undersigned Judge of said Court that the
Writ of Habeas Corpus ought to issue.

     THEREFORE, IT IS ORDERED that a Writ of Habeas Corpus issue out
of and under the seal of said Court directed to the Honorable E. F. Schubert,
M. D., Superintendent of Central State Hospital, located in Waupun, Dodge

ILCOX. RUDOLPH,
BASTA & RATHJEN
ATTORNEYS AT LAW
P.O. BOX O
AUTOMA, WIS. 54982

County, Wisconsin, commanding him to produce the body of the said Edward Gein before me in the courtroom of said Court in the Waushara County Court House at Wautoma, Wisconsin, on the 27th day of June, 1974, at 10:00 o'clock A. M. in the forenoon of said day, to do and receive what shall then and there be considered concerning the said Edward Gein and that the said Edward Gein shall be brought to Waushara County on June 26, 1974, for the purpose of a conference with his attorney, and to have then and there said Writ.

Dated at *Milwaukee*, Wisconsin, this *19th* day of June, 1974.

BY THE COURT:

R. H. Gollmar, Circuit Judge

-2-

STATE OF WISCONSIN   CIRCUIT COURT   WAUSHARA COUNTY
- -

In the Matter of the Mental Condition of

       EDWARD GEIN   **PETITION FOR WRIT**

Heretofore Adjudged to be Mentally Ill.

- -

TO THE SAID COURT:

      The petition of Robert P. Rudolph, Special Prosecutor for the State of Wisconsin, County of Waushara, respectfully represents:

      That the above named patient, Edward Gein, is now confined and committed as a patient to the Central State Hospital at Waupun in Dodge County, Wisconsin, as a result of being adjudged mentally ill by the Circuit Court of Waushara County, Wisconsin, on the 15th day of November, 1968.

      That a re-examination in relation to the aforementioned commitment has been scheduled for June 27, 1974, at 10:00 o'clock A. M. before the said Waushara County Circuit Court; and that said examination must be had in the presence of the patient.

      Your petitioner, therefore, prays that a Writ of Habeas Corpus be issued and directed to E. F. Schubert, M. D., Superintendent of Central State Hospital at Waupun, Wisconsin, commanding that he have the body of said patient, Edward Gein, before the said Court to do and receive what shall then and there be considered concerning the said patient.

      Dated: _____June 17_____, 1974.

                            _____
                            Robert P. Rudolph, Special
                            Prosecutor for the State of Wis-
                            consin, County of Waushara.

ILCOX, RUDOLPH,
BASTA & RATHJEN
ATTORNEYS AT LAW
P.O. BOX O
WAUTOMA, WIS. 54982

STATE OF WISCONSIN)
)ss.
COUNTY OF WAUSHARA)

     Robert P. Rudolph, being first duly sworn on oath, deposes and
says that he has read the above and foregoing petition, and knows the contents
thereof, and that the same are true to his own knowledge except as to those
matters stated upon information and belief, and as to such matters he believes
the same to be true.

Robert P. Rudolph
_____
        Robert P. Rudolph

Subscribed and sworn to before me
this _17th_ day of _June_ , 1974.

Renee Miller
_____
Renee Miller, Notary Public, Wis.
My commission expires May 16, 1976.

Chapter 8

Address of Sites

Addresses to Sites

Ed Gein's Land: N5691 2nd Ave, Plainfield, WI

Bernice Worden Home: 538 W. North St., Plainfield, WI

Worden Hardware Store: 110 S. Main St., Plainfield, WI

Frank Worden Home: 226 Poplar St, Plainfield, WI

Plainfield Methodist Church: 308 N. Main St. Plainfield, WI

Plainfield Cemetery: 6590 5th Ave, Plainfield, WI

Spirit Land Cemetery: 6527 Hwy D, Almond, WI

Hancock Cemetery: N3800 4th Ave, Hancock, WI

Mary Hogan's Bar: 140 Hwy D & Elm Rd, Bancroft, WI

Lester & Irene Hill: N6520 3rd St. Plainfield, WI

Goult's Funeral Parlor: 120 W. North St, Plainfield, WI

Waushara County Court House: 209 St. Marie St., Wautoma, WI

Old Waushara County Jail: 209 St. Marie St., Wautoma, WI

Ed's home where born: 612 Gould St, La Crosse, WI

1931 Home: 1931 Wood St, La Crosse, WI

Another Gein home at 1899: 1032 St. Charles St., La Crosse, WI

A. Gein Mercantile: 914 Caledonia St, La Crosse, WI

Final Thoughts

The following comments are of my own opinion after hours of research into the history of Ed Gein. One of the first questions people have asked me about Ed is "was he a cannibal and did he ever have sex with his victims"? My answer has always been no. After going over all the interviews the police and psychologists had with Ed Gein, I noticed that Ed always seemed to tell the truth. Now he did admit to trying to have sex with Bernice Worden's body, but he could not achieve an erection. He also admitted that the bodies smelled bad of embalming fluid.

Another question people have asked me about was how Ed Gein got the idea of making things out of human skin and remains.

Ed Gein was an avid reader of true crime and World War 2 atrocities the Germans did to the prisoners in the concentration camps. After the defeat of Nazi Germany, claims circulated that LIse Koch, wife of the commandant of Buchenwald concentration camp, had possessed lampshades made of human skin, and had specifically tattooed prisoners killed in order to use their skin for this purpose.

Ed's mother Augusta always wanted a daughter and when she decided to have a second child, she was disappointed when her son Ed was born and was not shy of telling him that. Ed always wanted to please his mother and therefore wanted to become a girl, so that is why he built the "skin suit", so he could be a girl.

Ed Gein will always be part of history and be linked to the town of Plainfield, Wisconsin. Unfortunately, that will never change for the people of Plainfield.

Made in the USA
Coppell, TX
29 May 2021